ZERO
TO
HERO

How I Went From Being A Losing Trader To A Consistently Profitable One

A TRUE STORY

YVAN BYEAJEE

To my younger brother Kevin.

CONTENTS

ABOUT THE AUTHOR

My name is Yvan Byeajee and I am the creator of Trading Composure, a blog where I share the many lessons I learned about trading, habits, beliefs, behavior, mindfulness, success, happiness, motivation, all of which are paramount if trading for a living is something you're interested in.

I started my trading journey in 2006. Over the course of the following 5 years or so, I went through significant drawdowns – both financial and emotional.

My repeated failures in the markets pushed me to question my role in the kind of results I was engineering for myself month after month, year after year.

Through this mere act of reflection and self-analysis came a whole new paradigm.

Said this way, it might seem like it was smooth sailing from there – it wasn't! But slowly (and eventually), I started to become more and more consistent.

2013 was my first profitable year as a trader. That is the year where I also came in 2nd in a live trading competition.

I started Trading Composure to share the lessons failure and hardship taught me and, today, I help people change their trading results through my work.

Thank you for purchasing this book. I hope you find it useful. If there's anything I can help with, I'm reachable at www.tradingcomposure.com

INTRODUCTION

We mold our own reality in the markets! Although hard to accept, this is an undeniable truth. Seen through the right angle, though, this truth can become quite liberating because if trading success is a function of how you perceive things and how you decide to act on that which you perceive, then I think it is safe to say that you have the power to change your trading results. You just have to work on yourself first.

But how do you change yourself so that you can start acting in your own best interest? How can you change your experience of trading in a way that is truly fulfilling? This book presents to you the answer! At its heart, it is straight forward and written in a manner that is easy to grasp – yet within its pages you will find rich information on why trading success appears so close, yet out of reach for most. I will give you a simple instruction on how to change your experience of trading in a way that makes your market goals attainable.

However, the only thing that will bring you the results is full commitment to the task that I describe. I wrote this book with the assumption that you desire durable trading success strong enough that you are willing to "erase" whatever conflicting beliefs you hold that would prevent you from consistently doing that task.

I am convinced that anyone can be a successful trader, and throughout the book, I will share with you some intimate and personal aspects of my story so as to better illustrate that point.

I hope that, whatever reasons have brought you to this book or have brought this book to you, you will find within it incomparable insights into the nature of your reality – in and out of the markets.

Yvan Byeajee

1 MY HUMBLE BEGINNINGS

The sun is starting to set as I write this first paragraph. I have an ocean view and I am currently in the Mascarenhas Archipelago on a tropical island called Mauritius, nearly half the size of Rhode Island. It is winter at the moment but that doesn't mean much here as the annual average temperature revolves around 26°C (76°F). Where I sit, the sand is golden, soft, but crisp, and as I gaze at the water, it is invitingly warm, transparent, with a display of various shades of turquoise. I feel so blessed to be here! It is surely a spiritual experience and at this very moment, I can only breathe mindfully as I contemplate my life and feel a great degree of appreciation for it.

Trading has given me the opportunity to experience a certain degree of freedom that most people can only dream of. It wasn't always like this, though. I struggled a lot before I was able to return consistent profits from my trading operations. There is no way I can deny that and the memories of those painful times still trigger a deep emotional response within me. But I intimately believe now that some of our most painful experiences happen for a reason. They are here to teach us something about ourselves, notably how inflexible we are to changes. I am grateful for the painful experiences, especially when I came to realize my role in it. I would not change a moment of it, though I never wish to repeat them.

My original choice for the title of this book was "Equilibrium: How I calmed my mind and improved my trading results", however I decided to go with a title that did a better job at appealing to the masses. Empirically, people, in general, are more inclined to buy books with "get rich quick" titles, so my intention was to touch as many people as I possibly could with my story – which is one of hard work, dedication, pain, but also spiritual awakening and self-realization.

Trading is not a get rich quick endeavor! It could be but if you get in for the wrong reasons, chances are that you will end up disappointed. So, I think it is important to have a real discussion, based on integrity and intellectual honesty, about the implications of trading for a living. From my own experience, durable success in the markets is a function of the kind of habits you cultivate on a daily basis. When I first started out, like most people I had no clues of what it really meant to trade for a living. I knew there would be some hard work, dedication and sacrifice involved but I didn't know to what extent.

To have you fully understand where I have been and how I can help you better evolve in your own journey, I think it is best that I start from the beginning. My interest for financial markets coincidentally started when I became old enough to understand the necessity of having a substantial amount of money in order to have a good life. I remember my older brother showing me a financial website and eagerly saying "people actually make a living buying and selling stocks on a regular basis, you know –

and you can too!" I don't know whether his intentions were to tease me or not, but I was struck with curiosity. I started researching more on the subject; though, I can't say that this research was fructuous. Those were the early days of the internet and trading-related information wasn't readily accessible within the click of a mouse, nor was it as inexpensive or free as it is nowadays. Yet, the modicum of information that I found sparked my interest even more, firmly planting the trading/ investing seed inside my head.

I was so fascinated by compound return tables, quotes, and market-related news, still I could not understand how one could find information or learn something from the enormous amount of numbers, symbols, and names that did not mean anything to me at all. But I was determined to learn!

Fast forward a couple of years, I had accumulated a rather significant amount of money from various jobs I took throughout the years, and I was finally ready to trade. I can still recall my state of mind at that time – a subtle combination of excitement, eagerness, hope, but also delusions as to what was realistically possible in terms of returns in the markets. Making money in trading surely seemed "easy" – just like a low hanging fruit waiting to be plucked. So I thought!

For a very long time, I couldn't manufacture consistent results from my trading operations. While I did make money here and there, I almost always ended up giving back those profits to the markets one way or the other – plus more! Pretty ironic, isn't it? I embarked on this journey to financial independence but all I got in return were losses; the drawdowns were not only financial but emotional as well.

Trading, like any high-performance endeavor, is a

mental game where we are required to pay attention to the present moment. But this is not enough! We have to stay present in a way that ensures that we execute our methodology flawlessly so that our results are in line with its capabilities. In other words, we have to learn to dissociate ourselves from our thoughts and feelings!

The character of this conversation we are constantly having with ourselves is, by and large, what engineers our trading results, our unhappiness, and the mediocrity of our lives in the present moment. Therefore, it becomes clear that the amount of money we accumulate in the markets isn't solely a function of how much time we spend exposing ourselves to the opportunities – it is also a function of our state of mind.

Early in my trading career, I didn't think of trading as a performance-based endeavor where you have to be on top of your mental form day-in, day-out. Like most, I came into this business with my backpack of insecurities, denied impulses, bad habits, fears, cravings... thinking that I would make it as a consistently profitable trader without a profound work on myself. Little did I know that by being mentally unprepared, I was actually preparing to fail. It's only when I was faced with mediocre results months after months, year after year, that I finally got it: something was out of whack with the way I approached trading.

The primary reason was that I was all too logical and numbers-oriented in my approach because I thought that was the key to success. I had completely ignored the psychological aspect of the game as I assumed that I had the innate mental skills to trade successfully, or that I had a god given talent that would make me prevail over the thousands of other participants who fail in this field. Welcome to the human condition! We all think that things are going to be different for us but it is rarely the case.

The other reason why I failed over and over (and over) again was because I was too much in my head. I would over-think the trades that I placed and the ones that I didn't. I would let winners go to my head and losers to my heart. I would constantly spare in weighing, doubting, judging... I felt identical to my inner states, and this affected my bottom line results for the simple reason that I almost always ended up acting on those thoughts and feelings.

We all have this chatter happening within the confines of our minds, always voicing its opinions, moods, and states. It is a voice that can reassure but more often than not it disparages. That is what it does best, and above all it just never shuts up! Buddhists call this voice "The monkey mind" – it is the mind that all humans possess and the mind that we, traders, have to learn to tame in order to unleash our true potential. I have learned to tame my inner voice and so can you!

2 THE SHIFT

While a statistically tested strategy and an efficient money management technique are primordial, the right mindset is what glues everything together. The reason for that is rather simple: Trading is a very tough profession as it requires us to take quick and often counter-intuitive decisions. And most of the time the quality of these decisions is affected by myriads of factors based on our current mental state — are we sad, happy, anxious, depressed; are we hungry, tired... These decisions will also involve all of our beliefs about money, certainty, failure, right and wrong, and so on. When you are forced into making quick decisions, if you are incognizant and unaware of your inner states, the strongest thoughts, feelings, or emotions are going to prevail. So to succeed as a trader, we need a certain presence of mind and an awareness of our inner states.

If you do not sort out your psychological shortcomings, durable market success will always seem elusive because an impulsive move based on your dysfunctional beliefs, unresolved emotional pain, thoughts, or feelings will always be right around the corner waiting to sap days, weeks or months of hard earned profits.

The fundamental idea behind trading is that it is a game where we are rewarded for our ability to mindfully abide by a certain set of tested rules. Said this way, it surely sounds easy – it's not! If you are reading this book, chances are that you have already traded before, so you know exactly what I'm talking about.

But "not easy" does not mean "impossible." There is nothing esoteric or even illusory about trading success. In most cases it just requires an openness to challenge your current set of behaviors and select the most appropriate set of steps that provides better psychological satisfaction. In other words, there is a way to trade that offers better psychological well-being in the long run. And my argument to you is that you have been trading with an apprehension to short-term pain while seeking short-term emotional gratification. To trade successfully, you have to turn this around: Embrace the short-term pain and seek long-term emotional gratification!

Everything we do in life is for the purpose of altering the way we feel. We form relationships so that we can feel certain emotions – maybe love, and avoid others, like loneliness. We eat specific foods to enjoy their ephemeral presence on our tongues. We read for the pleasure of thinking another person's thoughts. The brain is a pleasure-seeking machine – we usually do what makes us feel good. In trading, this natural tendency of always chasing pleasure, as opposed to pain, is often counter-productive just because of the way financial markets are designed to make profits available for us.

What makes us feel good and steer away from short-term emotional pain is usually the wrong decision to take.

For example, taking profits early by fear of losing all; removing a stop-loss because of some memories we have of past trades that could have worked well if we gave them a little more space; risking more than we should on any single trade; buying at the top and selling at the bottom, these things surely feel psychologically good at first, until their negative repercussions unfold. Acknowledging that this is the structure of the game we are playing allows us to play it differently.

Doing what is difficult over what is easy is a skill that we can learn, and how we pay attention to the present moment largely determines our ability to cultivate and apply that skill. By that same token, it allows us to trade our set of rules efficiently, thus returning consistent results out of our trading operations.

When we are able to practice patience instead of giving into our instant pleasure seeking nature; when we are able to cultivate equanimity instead of impulse driven behaviors, we allow ourselves to experience better psychological satisfaction. But that is not all. We also largely change the character of our experiences and, therefore, the quality of our lives.

What can be expected, if such a behavior is practiced and refined, is the learning of enjoying the struggle. In other words, when we keep doing things that are in our best interests – as hard as it is to do those things – slowly our minds start to create new neural pathways, thus new associations, consequently linking the mental struggle to the ensuing pleasure of having consistent trading results.

If you have been to the gym before, you must know first-hand that certain kinds of pain can be exquisitely pleasurable. The burn of lifting weights, for instance, would be agonizing if it was a symptom of terminal illness.

But because it is associated with health and fitness, most people find it enjoyable. Similarly, we can come to a point in our trading where the mental discomforts we experience as a result of doing what we should do instead of what we want to do, becomes synonymous to positive returns over a set number of trades.

I think we can never completely rid ourselves of the emotions that come along with trading. At the time of this writing, I have been trading for 8 years now, and I still can't figure out what it means to "control emotions" as we often hear traders preach on the internet – if by this logic, "emotional control" suggests eliminating or suppressing emotions. Personally, I still experience that gut churning feeling when price gaps below my stop loss. I still experience that acute feeling of frustration when I am out of a trade with small gains while being witness to the explosion of price right after I'm out. I still have "what ifs" thoughts popping into my consciousness every now and then. Of course, to a much lesser degree now, but these thoughts, sensations, and feelings, they never completely disappear regardless of one's commitment or level of expertise. And there is a very logical reason for that: Emotions are simply embedded in our human nature. Simply stating that one could trade without emotions is like saying that one could go about without having thoughts. It's impossible!

The good news is that the possibility exists to completely drop thoughts, feelings or emotions. This is not to say that they do not occur in consciousness – they still do and they always will. But with experience and the right practice you can learn not to feel identical to everything that goes on in your mind and body. In other words, you don't associate yourself with them anymore; you become a passive observer of your own thoughts, feelings, and sensations, in such a way that they do not impinge on your behavior anymore. By means of observation, you become detached from them!

The most important questions that struggling traders need to ask themselves are these: "How do I create consistency?" "How do I change my experience of trading to something that is truly fulfilling?" Notice how those questions involve the self. This shows us that "We" are the key to the trading conundrum! If our experience of trading isn't satisfactory to us as a result of how we perceive and do things, then we have to change our approach to trading in favor of a way that is more satisfying to us. This shift has to come from within us because as much as we would want the markets to change and conform to what are inside of us in terms of inner occurrences, it's never going to happen. We cannot change the markets, we can only change ourselves! This openness to ask the right questions and change ourselves is sine qua non.

There is an important caveat, though: An openness to learn shouldn't strip us from a healthy dose of skepticism that prevents us from taking anything and everything for granted – which may lead us down unproductive paths. There are tons of E-books on the subject of trading psychology that oversimplify things too much that they leave the real and important questions unanswered. In this day and age of technology and social Medias, it is easy to sit on your couch, share motivational quotes, talk the talk, instigate a nice database of followers, and start selling courses and e-books "effortlessly." However, when one scrutinizes a little bit (usually through experience) it becomes clear that those contents are based on rehashed platitudes and even fallacies. Plus, those people rarely walk the talk themselves however much they try to impress with their credentials. And in any way, if they did follow what they preach it would have been clear to them that the information they share sometimes is based on unsound principles.

Wisdom is nothing more than the ability to follow one's own pieces of advice, and what I talk about in this book I practice, not once a week, not once in a while, but every single day.

I do not pretend to know everything there is to know about the mental aspect of trading. In fact, I don't have any credentials in psychology; however, I learned most of what I discuss in this book through repeated mistakes, painful losses, and failures. The mind is seen as this perplexing and peculiar place that can only be understood by experts (psychologists), but my argument is that we don't need a Ph.D. to understand its nature. We just have to make ourselves available to learning more about the nature of our experiences – and the daily practice I describe in this book helps us get there.

3 SELF ANALYSIS

Developing some strong self-analysis skills is the basis for any positive changes in your trading habits. To give you some context around this statement, picture this: I was raised in a rather unstable environment. My parents separated a couple of months after I was born. My childhood was mainly composed of moving around a lot – alternatively living with my mother, my uncle, my father, and then back with my mother. Growing up, there are not any memories in my mind of me sharing a beautiful moment with my mother. I never had the luxury of having a loving relationship with her. It was quite the opposite. I was raised by a woman with a narcissistic personality disorder, who replaced care and nurturing with neglect and uncertainty – who didn't have the capacity to love me. Sure she showed love to my older brother, her "right arm" as she used to call him. He was the Golden Child and could do no wrong while I was merely the scapegoat. I was constantly compared to him and my inadequacy was thrown at my face on a near daily basis.

Looking back on our family dynamics it makes me feel

like I was a slave in a sheltered world of narcissism, racism, prejudice, abuse... My teenage years were some of the most difficult periods of my life where I was in search of who I am, my purpose, what drives me, etc., and I needed support and direction during that time. All I got was confinement, isolation, verbal assaults, humiliation, intimidation, infantilization, and other treatments which contributed to the diminishment of my sense of identity, dignity, and self-worth. The negative energy that I accumulated from these mistreatments needed to be canalized and evacuated, so in turn, I ended up hurting my younger brother insofar as I was being hurt myself. This is what hurts me the most nowadays, it's the harm that I have inflicted upon my younger brother who never deserved that. In my quest to understand why my own mother would impose such a cruel treatment on my own person, I had become oblivious to the fact that part of me became her!

One day, you finally wake up as an adult and you realize that this abusive and highly toxic environment has consequences. In addition to being unable to love myself, I experienced lots of difficulties with self-control and self-regulation. I became more and more introverted and closed off, and I inherited an array of dysfunctional beliefs that affected the way I perceived myself and experienced my life. I was taught to fear failure and to reject being wrong. I was taught to be a pathological perfectionist, and to have an excessive love for money and material possessions – as if my happiness was contingent upon those things.

This is not to say that my condition was unique, all of us suffer from those dysfunctional beliefs to different degrees. Just the mere fact that we evolve in a world where losers and failures are marginalized; where our self-worth is a function of our net worth, and where absolute perfection is the norm, is conducive to the formation and perpetuation of those beliefs. I am not going to dive into why those beliefs are dysfunctional in nature as I express it in my other book, Paradigm Shift, but the one thing that I want you to take from this is that specific beliefs have specific consequences. The set of beliefs I described is highly incompatible with successful trading, and being raised in such an unstable environment ensured that those beliefs grew out of proportions in me.

Years later, I found some perspective as an adult when I moved out of the house, but still the abuse I had experienced during the earlier parts of my life stuck with me. So I unknowingly continued to abuse myself emotionally and mentally. There was so much unresolved suffering in my life, and in my past, that I was carrying them into the present moment. I didn't know how to heal those wounds, and I lived life intimately thinking that I wasn't a valuable human being. When the people you trust the most treat you with such indignity, at some point you are bound to believe that something is wrong with you. Unfortunately, as years went by I crafted my life around those thoughts, and I attracted people and experiences that proved me that I was right in my assessment of reality.

Naturally, when I started trading and encountered losses, it insidiously revived some painful moments of my past where I felt unworthy and inadequate. It's as if those losses tapped into that reserve of negatively charged mental energy that never went away, always waiting to resurface when triggered.

Later in my career, I developed a statistical edge in the markets and a sound risk and money management technique, but still I couldn't get myself to execute that methodology flawlessly. I froze, as thoughts of failures prevented me from pulling the trigger on what could have been lucrative trades in hindsight. I would internalize every market action making it a right or wrong game. If I was wrong, I would consider it as an attack on my ego and I would take unwarranted entries in an attempt to get back the money lost. I wanted to feel whole again! If I was right, I would feel invincible, thus taking on excessive risk. To put it another way, I was an emotional mess – a walking time bomb waiting to blow up my account!

The constant over-thinking and over-attachment to my story made trading a very frustrating and exasperating endeavor for me. Additionally, I was in poor health. The chronic stress of unresolved emotional pain wreaked havoc on my immune system, circulatory system, cardiac function, hormone levels, and other physical functions. As years went by – as I kept trading – I was becoming more and more unhappy. I felt I hit rock bottom in September 2011 when I had lost 90% of my trading account after spending 5 years losing money in the markets. I was left broke and broken!

My lack of success almost drove me out of trading. I remember being dragged out of bed one night by the overwhelming chatter in my mind. It's as if the purpose of that inner "voice" was to undermine me at all cost. I was sweating profusely and I felt a deep sense of numbness in the pit of my stomach while at the same time a despair for which I cannot seem to express accurately with words. At that particular moment, I thought to myself, "I can't do this anymore. I just can't. There has to be a better way!" I didn't sleep for the rest of the night; I stayed in bed, laid on my side balled into a tight grip, prisoner of my inner conditions.

The ensuing days I took a break from the markets – I could barely get myself to look at my trading account because I was so afraid of what I would see there. At one point I went to a park and I sat on a bench. Summer had just ended; leaves were starting to fall, and the area, usually lively and colorful, was deserted and bleak. I felt empty, but as I sat down to ruminate on the mediocrity of my existence, something else happened.

I saw a squirrel jump from one tree to another, from what appeared to be an amazing feat because the distance between the two trees was significant. Additionally, the branch that squirrel was on initially was so thin that it boggled my mind as to how that squirrel managed to jump from it without losing balance and velocity. I thought that the squirrel must have had the innate ability to gauge probabilities. It is just something that is built within them; they don't have to think about it, they just do it, naturally! This line of thinking, somehow, led me to think about the many commonalities between great traders. It became clear to me that these commonalities were not so much in the way they traded – in fact, not at all. Every single one of them used a different trading methodology from the other. But what they did share in common was their overall view of what a market is and what is possible within it. They began to treat it as a set of probabilities rather than possibilities.

That was the first part of a chain of epiphanies for me. It is not so much that I didn't know this fact before because I did. However, there is a difference between knowing something and believing something. All that time, that which I knew didn't hit me because I wasn't prepared yet to really understand it. I looked at the markets with eyes of wonder, desire, hope, so much that it obscured my vision. And the reality is that good traders do not see the markets this way at all. They recognize the overall opportunities inherent to trading, but they also realize that the way to get positive results is through the consistent execution of their proven methodology. In other words, they forget the possibilities and they focus strictly on the probabilities.

This approach ensures that they can trade their methodology with the least amount of emotional involvement because it prevents them from internalizing market action. By focusing on the probabilities, like the squirrel, they can completely immerse themselves in the present moment – body and mind.

A common platitude that we all hear and try to apply is not to trade emotionally. This is fine in theory, but how do we do that when it is in our very nature to feel emotions? The human animal is an emotionally-driven machine, and we can no more stop having emotions than we can stop breathing. We can no more stop thinking than we can stop feeling. All that we can aspire to do is to reduce the emotional implication and the thinking – the weighing, judging, doubting – to the bare minimum. This is definitely in the realm of what is possible, and thinking in probabilities is the first step that gets us there.

Then we can learn to adopt an observer stance; we can learn to detach ourselves from thoughts and emotions. The over-identification with our thoughts and emotions is what makes us shoot ourselves in the foot, so when we learn to separate ourselves from those inner occurrences, we free our potential as traders – but also as individuals.

Good traders have learned at one point in their career to free their minds of the emotional implications associated with mistakes and failures. They are flexible and have learned to thrive in uncertain environments, just like reeds that bend with the winds without breaking. They are not overly attached to money and the absolute need to be right. In turns, this engineers the kind of market performance they enjoy year after year.

For a very long time, I was very far from that ideal, but recognizing it was a huge step forward in my journey as a trader. All that time, I didn't think there was anything wrong with the way I approached trading. That is the way I approached everything in life, my relationship with money, people, work, etc. On any particular day, if I experienced a loss in the markets (realized or unrealized), it would negate everything good that happened to me on that specific day. Likewise, when I had a bad day, if I had a winner in the markets, this would instantly lift me, extracting me from my pain and misery to a state of ecstasy, excitement, and optimism. I clung, grasped, always seeking happiness and well-being outside of myself.

The hope that "the big one" was right around the corner was a thought I held dear. The idea was that such a trade would bring in enough profits to cover all my previous losses while allowing me to take some well-deserved vacations. Who knows, maybe there would be enough left to buy a nice car... and a beautiful Rolex watch? I love watches! This would surely provide me with an elongated sense of fulfillment and well-being.

Do you see how unhealthy this is? I am sure a lot of you experience this in your own lives. That is what happens when our well-being relies on processes that are out of our control – markets, money, or anything and anyone outside of ourselves. When we hand those the power to decide for us what we ought to feel in each and every moment, our mood swings from extreme to extreme like a pendulum. We lose control of ourselves, and we literally become drug addicts, always needing that buzz; that fill – and it's never enough; it's never satisfying.

Not many new traders focus on developing strong skills of self-analysis – in fact, most doubt that such abilities even exist. Yet, it is this capacity to trace our problem thoughts or emotions back, ultimately to some emotionally intense experience that led to us to learn some unskillful lessons, that determines our capacity to evolve beyond our limitations. When we become aware of our triggers, and the scripts they play over and over again, that awareness allows us to make choices we couldn't have conceived before.

Still on my break from trading, I started spending time with myself, sitting in random parks, trying to get a sense for my existence, its meaning, its purpose, and why still after all these years I wasn't able to succeed in the markets. I began investigating the nature of my thoughts, emotions, and memories. During that time, journaling became my best ally. The idea was to use the journal to keep a real-time record of anything that went through my mind; anything that could eventually lead me to understand why I was constantly sabotaging myself. When you have a pen and a piece of paper, and you are putting your thoughts down, it allows you to articulate clearly the thoughts in your mind and the feelings in your body that might just be hazy otherwise. When you have it on paper, it is not abstract anymore and you have something tangible to work with. At that point, writing becomes the catharsis of the mind.

Months passed and I gained more and more insights into my self-sabotaging behaviors. Now that I had a good understanding of what triggered my emotional responses to events and circumstances, I started searching for ways to help me rise above those inner "fetters", thus redefining my reality. What I stumbled across did exactly that!

4 THE MAGIC PILL

Suppose I tell you about a magic pill that you could take daily. That magic pill could drastically increase your ability to take rational decisions in the markets; it could reduce your anxiety when you trade; decrease impulsivity, and increase your overall capacity to act in your best interest in the markets. Would you take such a pill? Suppose further that the pill has a great variety of positive side effects like increased self-esteem, acceptance of the past, acceptance of the unknown, self-trust, improved memory, and so on. Suppose, finally, that the pill is all natural, but that is not all: It costs absolutely nothing... the only caveat is that you just have to be willing to take it every... single... day! Now would you still take it? That pill exists – it's called meditation.

The habit of meditation the most powerful thing I have ever learned. If I had to attribute my success in the markets to a habit that I do consistently in my day-to-day life, without a single ounce of hesitation I would say meditation.

The source of our problems – as traders – is the very thing that is our greatest asset: Our minds! Taking a trade too soon; taking it too late; not taking a signal at all; not putting a stop in; moving our stop; not taking profits, or taking too little of it, all these trading errors result from our thoughts. In fact, as a species, most of our dissatisfactions, worries, and pain are engineered by our thoughts. The good news is that we can learn to change our relationship with those states of the mind. The practice of meditation comes from a 2,500-year-old tradition of using an anchor like the breath to stabilize attention; cut through this constant association with our thoughts and feelings, and bring awareness to the present moment.

I was incredibly skeptical about meditation at first. Not only was I skeptical about anything bordering on the metaphysical, which I assumed meditation involved, but I also thought that it was strictly reserved for monks, ascetics, and other contemplatives. The thing that got me to open my mind just a crack was hearing about the science (see The studies section) and I think that is true for a lot of people who have given it a try of late. Naturally one hears about those extraordinary things meditation does to the brain and the body, and quickly it becomes all compelling. It seemed like the practice could provide some kind of answer to my problems, so I tried it.

I have to say, my first taste of it was miserable. I had set an alarm for forty minutes (not a very good idea if you are just starting out) and had a full-on collision with the zoo that is my mind. It was really hard to stay focused more than 5 seconds on my breath and at the end of that painful session, I got even more frustrated. I reflexively thought that my mind was somehow busier than everyone else's and that I couldn't possibly tame it. Intrinsically, the realization that I was lost in thought 99% of the time didn't hit me as something that was deeply perplexing.

What bothered me the most was that I thought meditation was a complete waste of my time.

We spend our lives lost in thoughts. That is the natural tendency of the mind. It ruminates; it jumps from thought to thought incessantly, from morning till night, from birth till death, giving us no rest for a moment. Most of these thoughts are not exactly invited, they just appear in consciousness, occupy our attention for a while, and then disappear, making place for others. The question is, what should we make of this fact? In the west, for a very long time, the answer has been "Not much." In the east, especially in contemplative traditions like those of Buddhism, being distracted by thoughts is understood to be the very cause of human suffering.

In the Buddhist belief system, Siddhartha Gautama (the Buddha) is said to have attained enlightenment under the Bodhi Tree where he had been sitting in a meditative state for weeks. Soon after his enlightenment, he passed a man on the road who was struck by his extraordinary radiance and peaceful presence. The man stopped and asked: "You seem very special. What are you? Are you some kind of an angel?" "No," the Buddha replied. "Well, are you some kind of god then? You seem un-human." "No," he said. "Well, are you some kind of wizard or magician?" "No," he replied. "Well, are you a man?" "No." "Then what are you?" At this, the Buddha answered, "I am awake." In those three words, "I am awake", he gave the whole of Buddhist teachings.

The word "Buddha" means one who is awake. To my knowledge, Siddhartha Gautama wasn't some kind of deity or superhuman, although a lot of the beliefs attribute to him superpowers or a deistic nature. What most scholars agree upon is that he was just a human being who went on a quest to find the meaning of suffering – and he found his answers through his contemplative practice.

The practice of meditation does not ask us to become a Buddhist or a religious person. That is not the point here. Rather it invites us to fulfill the capacity we each have as humans to awaken – from this dream-like state we seem to all unconsciously be prisoners of.

Being analogous to thoughts is similar to being asleep and dreaming. It is a mode of not knowing what is going on in the present moment. Consider what happens in dreams: you fall asleep, and then all of a sudden you find yourself wandering in a park. The next second you are swimming in the ocean, in the company of a whale – and the mind doesn't even blink. It seems to have no expectations of continuity. The most surprising thing about dreams is certainly our lack of surprise when they arise. A similar thing happens to us with our thoughts when we are awake. We will tell ourselves the same thing 15 times in a row. We will doubt, comment, criticize, weigh, and judge anything and everything. Just imagine if other people could hear your thoughts broadcasted on a speaker all day long. You would seem completely insane! Upon close inspection, one could even call it a form of psychosis.

We spend our lives feeling identical to our thoughts. It doesn't matter if your mind is wandering over why the markets did what they did; the latest celebrity gossips, or what you had for lunch today... if you are thinking without knowing that you are thinking, that is what it feels to be identical to thoughts.

Thoughts are important. They are part and parcel of our human lives. Our ability to think is at the very core of our evolution as a species. Our thoughts gave birth to arts, literature, science, philosophy, and so on. So clearly, the problem is not thoughts themselves but the state of thinking without being fully aware that we are thinking – and that very state is the cause of all our woes despite our capabilities as humans. It is the reason why success in the markets appears so elusive; so close yet out of reach. Thoughts drive your behaviors, emotions, and determine your future expression in the markets.

In essence, what I am stating is that we have to learn to use our minds in a way that engenders a greater degree of satisfaction and well-being. We enjoy real freedom only when we are able to still our minds – even for a few moments at a time. But disrupting the flow of thoughts might look like an infeasible feat; however, meditation can eventually lead us there. With practice we can learn to separate ourselves from our thoughts, resulting in a better appreciation of the present moment and a drastic reduction of our inherent psychopathologies.

Not to know that there are alternatives to being lost in thoughts is to be a kind of prisoner of sorts, a slave, as I have been for a very long time. Some of you may think happy and interesting thoughts all day long but I'm imagining that most of you are like me. So how do we deal with this? In my attempt to find that answer, I decided to head on a meditation retreat.

5 THE AWAKENING

People who haven't tried meditation have very little insight into how their minds are constantly thinking. And when you bring to their attention that their minds are noisy, it generally doesn't mean anything to them. When these people try to meditate, they have one of two reactions: Some are so restless and overwhelmed by doubts that they can hardly attempt the exercise. "What the hell am I doing here sitting with my eyes closed?" "What is the point of paying attention to the breath?" "I feel ridiculous sitting there like a statue."... Strangely, their resistance isn't remotely interesting to them. They come away, after only a few minutes, thinking that the act of paying close attention to their experience is pointless.

But then there are the people who have an epiphany, where the unpleasant realization that their minds are digressing all over the place provoke the desire for further inquiry. Their inability to pay sustained attention to anything becomes interesting to them. And, they recognize it as impeding, despite the fact that almost everyone is in the same condition. That is exactly the realization that occurred to me the second time I tried meditation.

It seems taboo in most spiritual circles (especially in Buddhism) to make claims about one's own realization or "enlightenment"; however I think this does a disservice to everyone because it allows people to remain confused about how to practice and what they're looking for in this practice. So I will describe my experience...

I was so desperate with my life. My failures in the markets were the last drop that brought me on the verge of doing something so horrible that I now quiver just by the thought of it. In a quest to find some direction in my life, I attended a silent meditation retreat. I had nothing to lose so I thought to myself, "Might as well..."

The first few days into the retreat were excruciating, to say the least! The acute pain in my back as a result of all that sitting was analogous to being stabbed repeatedly with a sharp knife in that one specific area. It felt like I was beaten up and then forced to sit there in this crossed legged position. On top of that, my mind was a complete mess! I was such in a bad place physically and mentally that I was just about to get up, pack my stuff and leave. However, to this day, I still don't know what made me stay, but what I do know is that this decision profoundly changed something in me. It is as if this act of staying showed to my unconscious mind that I was finally ready for change.

At one point, right in the middle of meditation, unable to calm my mind, I thought of all my past mistakes and failures, whether they were trading-related or not. I got angry and frustrated at myself, so much that tears started dripping from my eyes. Right then, at that very moment, I had a great epiphany: How did these feelings and mental occurrences assert so much control over me? With great curiosity, I began watching them swirl within me like a cyclone. A few moments into this observation I noticed something rather peculiar. I felt detached from those thoughts and feelings of anger, frustration, despair – as if emancipated from them. I still felt the feelings swirl within me, but since I was merely observing them they didn't seem to have any control over me. They didn't bother me anymore!

I, then, experienced a deep peace settling within and soon enough my uncomfortable feelings began to dissipate, just like a cyclone loses its intensity and slowly fades away with time. Thoughts disappeared leaving space for breath – and only breath! I felt "empty", but in a good way. And, when thoughts finally came back again, I felt I was beneath them – in other words, I didn't feel identical to them, I was merely an observer of them.

All my life my thoughts defined who I was because I was unconsciously granting them permission to have power over me. This was my wellspring of torment and I never thought that there was an alternative to that. But at that very instant, I intimately knew I was onto something big and potentially life-changing!

Thoughts are necessary and we couldn't navigate our lives without them. But this automaticity of being lost in discursive thoughts and not knowing that you are thinking is the primary cause of human suffering because thoughts drive behavior, emotions, and each subsequent train of thought. When we are unaware of what we are thinking, this directly impacts the way we respond to everything that is outside of us. In trading, this is the reason why we cannot execute properly without making a number of trading errors. Meditation is simply a tool that allows us to "step back" to that process and discover the space in consciousness underneath this stream of thoughts.

After the retreat, eager to deepen my understanding of myself and how I essentially created my own pain and suffering in trading (but also in my personal life), I began cultivating a regular meditation practice. Slowly, it all began to make sense – my life's purpose, my past experiences, my failures in the markets... I began to see clearly how my beliefs and the over-identification with my thoughts created my reality. The attachment to a painful past created my experience of the present. My strong desire of always wanting to be right created my results in the markets and my craving for control and certainty made me inflexible, therefore, unable to adapt to changes. But now, I finally knew how to deal with those afflictive inner conditions. This breakthrough showed me that it was possible to release myself from my mental prison and transcend my disparaging and discursive mental chatters. I experienced it once at the retreat and although brief, it was the most relieving thing I had ever experienced – and I knew this experience was available for me to reproduce!

There is an alternative to being at the mercy of the next neurotic thought that comes careening into consciousness. There is an alternative to being forced into this boring and unproductive conversation we are constantly having with ourselves – this voice inside our heads telling us what we should have done, could have done; how we like this, and not that; how this is good, and this bad. When we break this spell, an extraordinary kind of relieve is expelled. Soon you begin to notice why you suffer; how you suffer; the mechanics of it from moment to moment; the mechanics of worry and doubt; fear, anger, etc. Meditation is a tool to relax that automaticity, but that tool can be hard won because it is not easy to meditate.

Paying attention to the breath without getting lost in thought is a simple instruction, indeed, but incredibly difficult to perform at first. However, just like with anything, a regular practice allows you to develop your capacity to do it – and there is an incredible freedom that comes with that! It is just a relief to be able to put down the burden of your rumination, if only for a few moments. Furthermore, what is particularly interesting is that it breaks a fundamental cognitive illusion that most of us live with. This illusion is this sense of "self" that we live with. It is that feeling of being a passenger inside our body. If this breakthrough happens, even for a short moment, the psychological benefits are tremendous.

6 THE SELF: A CONSTRUCT!

There are truths to be known about the human condition and my argument is that certain of these truths are worth knowing. They can not only help us get more consistent results in trading but also live better lives. For instance, not to know that our sense of "self" is an illusion is to be a sort of prisoner. This feeling of being an ego; a passenger living in a body, an "I", is a direct result of myriads of neurophysiological processes in the brain that we have no control over.

Upon close inspection, it is possible to lose this feeling of "self" that is the center of experience. For thousands of years, people have claimed that they were able to do so through meditation. Rather than having the experience of being a locus of consciousness in the head, looking at a world that is separate from what you are, you can just be at one with everything that is experienced. This is classically described as self-transcendence, and the realization only came to me much later that it was this psychological state that I experienced during the retreat. Candidly, this experience blew my mind and it took me months to integrate the understanding of this possibility into my intellectual life.

While I don't believe that cutting through that feeling of "I" reveals to us some kind of secrets about the possible existence of a god (or gods), because objectively speaking, I haven't experienced such insights, it does tell us a lot about the nature of our minds. And that is a fact. We spend 99% of our time lost in thoughts, and this engineers for the most part our suffering on this earth. Meditation allows us to escape that mental prison in such a way that it becomes clearer to us that the way we think directly influences our experience of the world. It shows us that there is more to our experiences than what our thoughts suggest.

Our consciousness is intrinsically free of this feeling of self. In fact, as you develop some strong skills of introspection; when you pay attention, soon you begin to see that consciousness beneath that sense of self is pure and void of duality, biases, opinions, ideas – it is merely an observer of those states. Consciousness is what it feels like to be you; it is that which is merely aware of everything. And that which is aware of frustration is not frustrated. That which is aware of anger is not angry. That which is aware of fear is not fearful. That which is aware of an impending impulse is not impulsive. There is a tremendous amount of relief to be had when you train yourself to sink beneath your thoughts and feelings and sensations. However, once you become lost in those afflictive states, again you lose that clarity of perception. So, the awareness of the space beneath your incessant thoughts and emotions is a practice that ought to be cultivated over and over again throughout the day. And it could take the form of three simple mindful cycles of breath every now and then.

Just try this for a minute:

Close your eyes. Think of a good trade that you placed—visualize the moment when you exited that trade and how you felt. Notice how the mere thought of that past evokes a feeling in the present. Pause for a second. Breathe! Feel that space beneath your thoughts. Feel what it is like to be you beneath the thoughts. This is consciousness – pure and empty. It is the observer! Now, does consciousness itself feel happy? Is it truly changed or affected by what it knows? No. Thoughts and emotions arise in consciousness the way clouds appear in the blue sky. The sky is always there. Clouds (thoughts, emotions) come and go, and the sky merely witnesses to them.

Now think of something unpleasant: Perhaps you exited another trade with significant losses. Or maybe there was a trade that you didn't take because you were feeling acutely anxious about it. Notice whatever feelings arise in the wake of these thoughts. They are also appearances in consciousness. Do they have the power to change what consciousness is in and of itself? No. Consciousness is merely aware of those feelings.

There is real freedom to be found in this simple practice of paying attention to yourself because if you catch yourself being angry, frustrated, hesitant, fearful... at any moment when you realize that you are merely observing those states, the choice not to act on them becomes clear. You can choose to let them fade away instead of pressing on them. They don't have to prevent you from doing what you really know you have to do for the sake of your long term results.

But you are unlikely to find that freedom without looking carefully into the nature of consciousness, again and again. Although that state of self-transcendence is available for us to experience on a moment-to-moment basis, it is hard won. Our mind's main job is to think!

Notice how thoughts keep arising even while reading this page. I'm sure your attention has certainly drifted several times. Such wanderings of mind are natural and meditation doesn't entail the suppression of thoughts. It does require though that we notice thoughts as they emerge and recognize them to be passing appearances in consciousness – just like clouds in the sky. In subjective terms, you are consciousness itself – you are not the next discursive words or images that appear in your mind. Not seeing them arise, however, you will automatically identify to them. In other words, the next thoughts arising in consciousness will seem to become what you are. But how could you actually be a thought? Whatever their content, thoughts vanish almost as soon as they appear.

If you can learn to separate yourself from your thoughts, nothing can prevent you from achieving the type of success you desire in the markets. Nothing! If you can escape the usual association to your thoughts of fear, anger, shame, despair; if you can learn to relieve yourself of the feeling that you call "I", even for a few moment at a time but reliably, one day you could, in theory, become the best trader that ever lived. No kidding! But then again you would certainly realize that this success doesn't mean much in the grand scheme of your life.

A lot of people spend their lives trying to find that ultimate freedom. They abandon everything, material possessions, loved ones, pleasures of this world, and they embark on a spiritual journey to find meaning, purpose,... to find themselves! While their reasons to do this are very valid, a permanent state of freedom is hardly earned. Personally, at my level of practice, this freedom from the self only lasts a few moments. But these moments can be repeated, thus punctuating ordinary experience. This has made all the difference in my life!

7 HOW TO MEDITATE

There are many ways we can practice meditation, and my own practice has evolved over time to fit my needs. I first started meditating in a Buddhist context; I have tried Vipassana, and until recently I practiced Zazen. Quite frankly, having practiced both rather intensively, I can say that they are essentially the same, as both use the breath as an anchor and both take you to greater heights of self-awareness. So the debate on which type of meditation is better is out of the scope of this book and regardless of the type of practice you decide upon, the aim is to just sit. You suspend all judgmental thinking and you let words, ideas, images, and thoughts pass by without getting involved in them. The aim is to try to focus on what is here and now.

The practice of meditation is simple to describe but not easily performed. Yet, a genuine transformation in one's perception of the world is within reach for each and every one of us. Cultivating a regular practice is the only thing that will lead to success.

As every beginning meditator soon discovers, distraction is the normal condition of our minds: Most of us topple... we plunge into our usual thoughts of past, future; maybe songs, images... During meditation, we are learning to wake up from these states of the mind. The goal is to come out of the trance of discursive thinking and to stop reflexively grasping at the pleasant and recoiling from the unpleasant so that we can enjoy a mind undisturbed by worry and effortlessly aware of the flow of experience in the present.

Instructions:

1. Find a quiet spot. It really doesn't matter where you sit as long as you can sit without being bothered for at least 15-20 minutes.

2. Sit in front of a wall. The wall is a metaphor for the difficulties we all face in life and sitting facing that wall allows us to face our difficulties. If we can cultivate equanimity while facing the wall, then nothing prevents us from doing the same thing when we are faced with difficulties in life. But, this is optional so don't be bothered if you don't feel like doing that.

3. Sit comfortably. How you position your body has a lot to do with what happens with your mind and your breath. You are free to choose whichever position you are more comfortable with. The most effective positioning for my body is the stable, symmetrical position of the seated Buddha. I use a zafu (a small pillow) to raise my behind just a little so that the knees can touch the ground. With my bottom on the pillow and two knees touching the ground, I form a tripod base that is natural, grounded and stable.

3. Put on a timer. If you are just starting out, 10-15

minutes will do. You can increase your time when you have been used to sitting for a while. My practice has evolved to a point where I now sit for 20 minutes in the morning and 30 minutes at night. And of course, as stated in the previous chapter, throughout the day I try to snap out of the usual association to thoughts and emotions by becoming aware of my breath.

4. Choose the positioning of your hands. In my own practice, I fold them in a position called the cosmic mudra. The right hand is held palm up holding the left hand which is also held palm up so that the knuckles of both hands overlap. The thumbs are lightly touching thus, the hands form an oval, which can rest two fingers below the belly button. The cosmic mudra is there to help turn your attention inward. Again, this is optional. Feel free to just place your hands on your thighs.

5. Gradually become aware of the sensations of sitting. How does it feel? How do you feel in your body? How does it feel on your back? How about your legs? Don't analyze, weigh or judge... just witness! Perhaps take a few deep breaths. Allow gravity to settle you right where you are. Gradually become aware of the process of breathing. Notice where you feel the breath – do you feel it at the tip of the nose or is it at the rising and falling of the belly? Feel the sensations, from the beginning of the inhalation to the pauses, and finally to the exhalation. Just simply cover your breath with your awareness. Let it come and go naturally. The moment you see that you are lost in thoughts, simply observe those thoughts, whether they are images; things you are saying to yourself; past, future, whatever it is, just observe! Notice the feelings that usually accompany them. Notice how they disappear, and then come back to the sensations of breathing. What are the sensations you feel in your body? Again, don't spare in judgment, simply observe. You will get lost in thoughts

41

again and again. It's totally fine. Notice! Observe. See how the quality of your breath is congruent with your state of mind.

Again, the object of this meditation exercise is to be able to make a clear distinction between the moments where one is fully present and his/her distracting thoughts. Typically, when we find ourselves in a distracting thought we simply acknowledge the thought, and then we go back to focusing on breathing. As you continue to do this exercise day in and day out – as you keep practicing – what you will find is that the amount of time that it takes for you to recognize and acknowledge a distraction will start to collapse. As it gets smaller and smaller, there will come a point where the distraction and the awareness of the distraction will become virtually simultaneous. At this point, you would have become an objective observer to our own stream of thoughts. You would have trained your mind to be more present.

This is particularly beneficial when trading the markets because the first step towards changing repetitive patterns of negative behaviors is to recognize them in real time as opposed to recognizing them in hindsight.

But the benefits don't stop there – and they do not only pertain to trading. As you keep practicing, you will find yourself being more engaged in your life, more present, and as a result more fulfilled... happier! There is a whole different world out there to be experienced as we liberate ourselves from our thoughts. There is a strong connection between happiness and spiritual wisdom, and it is more direct than most people suppose.

8 THE GREAT MEANING

Life The life of a human being is really something! Even in the best of times – no one close to us died; we might enjoy financial stability – at the level of our true intentions we are perpetually in search of happiness. We seek pleasant sights, sounds, tastes, attitudes, but our pleasures are by their very nature fleeting. So we are only finding temporary relief from our search. If we have a winning trade, this remains vivid and intoxicating for about an hour – maybe a day. The pleasures we experience when we have sex, eat our favorite foods, play with our kids, are impermanent and the best we can do is to merely reiterate them as often as we are able to.

At one point, when you become consistently profitable in the markets, the success you might be craving so much right now will not matter to you as much anymore – trust me, it becomes less and less impressive. Winning trades become boring, losing trades equally boring – not void of emotions, just boring! You will feel the need to reiterate that sense of striving for something you care about, and trading will not provide you with that anymore. There comes a point where it becomes just a means to an end.

Notice at this juncture that very few people are going to say, "oh, I'm done, I met all my goals, and now I am just going to sit down and do nothing." Even when things go as well as they can go, the search for happiness and the very drive to keep boredom and dissatisfaction away continues.

So in this context, many people have begun to wonder whether or not a greater and deeper form of well-being exists. A form of well-being that is not contingent upon merely reiterating one's pleasures and avoiding one's pain. Is there a form of happiness that exists in the midst of old age, before one's desires get gratified, in the very midst of life's vicissitudes, death, trading losses, etc..? I think this question lies in the periphery of everyone's mind.

For the longest time, I have been pondering on that question. And I challenge you to do so as well. Start observing your thoughts, your desires, your feelings, your behaviors... and become the observer of your own life. Believe me... by doing so you will discover many things about the nature of living.

What I have discovered over the years, after doing so much introspection, is that happiness is not a place you go to. Happiness is not a person; it is not a trade, it is not a successful career. Happiness is not a dream you achieve. Happiness just is! We can create lives that are truly worth living given that these lives ineluctably come to an end. And, the capacity for us to see those changes and to live those lives is largely dependent on the frame we put on the present moment.

No matter where you are and no matter what you do; no matter how you look and no matter how much or less you have, you will find fulfillment in your life the moment you drop your self-concerns and focus on what is here and now. If you are not happy in those specific situations; if you are not happy with what you have and with who you are now, you will not find happiness by merely reiterating your pleasures. You may delude yourself into thinking otherwise, but in the end, you will go back to feeling miserable and unfulfilled. If there is a form of happiness that exists that is not conditional, then it should be found in the present.

It is difficult for most of us to accept this fact because if we do, we will have to wake up and take responsibility for how we feel and for our actions. We will have to take responsibility for our own lives, and this is challenging, more so scary.

For those of you who are on this journey of self-discovery and self-mastery, as time goes by, and as you travel farther and farther in your journey, you will discover what happiness is all about – and what is not. You will see that it is not money; it is not big houses, shiny cars... It is not even found in people but rather in having a meaning, a purpose in life, larger than your sense of self.

It is always about giving, about sharing what is best about ourselves with others, because, when we do so, we offer others the possibility of happiness and well-being.

Nowadays, I find my purpose by living simply and by reducing my physical footprint on this earth. I also share a portion of my profits from my different endeavors to charity whenever the markets are good to me on any specific year. I find my purpose by writing and helping other traders not merely survive but make real changes in their trading because I know success in trading is possible for anyone. I am a living proof that anyone can do this. I don't have anything extraordinary... I don't possess any special talent. I am just a regular guy who didn't give up.

Conclusion

We live in a world of cause and effect and what constitutes the reality of our lives is determined by a long chain of prior causes which, for the most part, we couldn't possibly have any control over. However, once we realize that the present is all we have, we can work on making the most of it.

We all have our personal stories of how we ended where we are today, and our past, while painful at times can serve us as a springboard to better and more fulfilling experiences in the present. But that can only happen if we embrace the lessons it has to offer. This means accepting failures, losses, mistakes, harm done, harm received for what they are: Learning experiences! Intrinsically, these experiences are nondual, and we are the ones putting context behind them. When we learn to embrace those experiences, as they are, we take full control of our lives.

I will never escape the memories of my painful past and also how I was forced to test the limit of my endurance in the markets. But I have learned to understand those tough times enough to see them in a positive and useful light. There is no better teacher but experience itself. While I am still in the process of "repairing myself" from my childhood traumas, I can attest that the quality of my life, in comparison to what it was, has drastically improved. Not because I am now financially secure but for the simple reason that I am finally at peace with myself.

My trading has also greatly improved. In 2013, I finish 2nd in a live trading competition organized by Mercury Derivatives (a Hertshten Group Company) and its partners. Congruently, this was also my first profitable year in the markets as a retail trader. For that specific year, I was up 54% with a maximum drawdown of around 10%. In 2014, I returned a respectable 49% with a maximum drawdown of around 10% also. So far, 2015 is shaping up to be my third profitable year and I am currently up 23% with a maximum drawdown of 12% at the time of this writing. These results are based on my swing trading account. I am not counting my other smaller account where I do options and day trades – which I am also up on.

But my results and my accomplishments are not the point here, and I am merely stating them to illustrate a keynote: It is possible to simply drop your problems! If only for a few moments at a time, you can release the clinging to your past, what you think of yourself, your beliefs, and really enjoy what is truly present here, now, in this very moment. It is possible to get yourself to tune out the noise in your mind. When you learn to do so; when you lose your self-concern, the markets will cease to assault you. And instead of taking from you, they will start giving to you! Getting there requires a change in attitude; it requires a change in the attentiveness you pay to your experience of the present moment.

The reality of our existence is always right here and right now! It is always the case however much our mental energy is spent on thinking about the past, planning for the future; mitigating risks... If one truly takes the time to think about this, it becomes clear that this is one of the most liberating truths about the nature of the human mind that can be given to us to contemplate. In fact, I think there is probably nothing more important to understand in this world if you want to be happy.

The past is a memory – it is a thought arising in the present. The future is merely anticipated – it is another thought arising in the present. What we truly have is this very moment. But we spend most of our lives forgetting that truth, fleeing it... overlooking it. Even in the markets, we are always thinking about past trades, or fantasizing about future ones, and this disrupts our capacity to truly appreciate the beauty and the uniqueness of this current trade. We are always transposing on it our fears and hopes, and when it doesn't conform to our expectations, we become disappointed. We are always solving a problem in our minds, and we manage to never really connect with the present and find fulfillment there because we are continually hoping to become happy in the future. And that future never arrives!

Even when we think we are in the present moment, in some ways we are always looking over its shoulders, so to speak. We are always anticipating what is coming next.

We have to shift this automaticity of always repudiating our present moment experience... of always being lost in thoughts. If our goal is durable success in the markets, there is no more important step to take than this one! And meditation allows us to cut through this automaticity, leading us to that ideal mindset that will allow us to manifest not only consistency in our actions, but also physical, emotional, and spiritual well-being.

THE STUDIES

The meditation-and-the-brain research has been rolling in steadily for a number of years now. Although a lot of the earlier studies were flawed and yielded unreliable results, more recent reviews have pointed out many of these flaws with the hope of guiding current research into a more fruitful path. Research on the processes and effects of meditation is a growing subfield of neuroscience therefore, new studies are coming out just about every week to illustrate the now confirmed benefits of meditation.

A few of those benefits that are particularly pertinent to trading are as follows:

1. Meditation reduces the "monkey mind." One of the most interesting studies in the last few years carried out at Yale University found that mindfulness meditation decreases activity in the default mode network – the brain network responsible for mind-wandering and self-referential thoughts.

The default mode network (DMN) is active when we are not focusing on anything in particular; when our minds are just wandering from thought to thought, like a monkey jumping from branch to branch. This is where the Buddhist expression "Monkey mind" comes from – it refers to the incessant chatter that goes on in our heads. Since mind-wandering is typically associated with being less happy, ruminating, and worrying about the past and future, it is the "goal" of meditation to dial it down. And several studies have shown that meditation, through its quieting effect on the DMN, appears to do just this.

Eventually, when the mind does start to wander like it just naturally does, because of the new connections that form, meditators are better at breaking the spell of association. This is particularly significant for us traders as it allows us to reroute our attention to the present whenever we catch ourselves indulging in thoughts of past or future trades; wins or losses, or any kind of weighing, judging or doubting.

The ability to stay presently focused allows us to trade and manage our current positions to the best of our abilities. It allows us to see market action from an objective and impartial standpoint.

http://www.pnas.org/content/108/50/20254.short

2. Meditation decreases depression. Do you feel depressed when you lose in the markets? Do you tend to ruminate on why the markets didn't accommodate you? A study conducted in Belgium, involving a decent sample of 400 students (age 13 - 20), concluded that participants who followed an in-class mindfulness program reported a reduction in depression, anxiety, and stress. Moreover, these students were less likely to develop pronounced depression-like symptoms.

Another study, from the University of California, concluded that mindfulness meditation decreases ruminative thinking and dysfunctional beliefs in people who struggled with depression in the past. Yet another concludes that mindfulness meditation may be effective to treat depression to a similar degree as antidepressant drug therapy.

http://www.scientificamerican.com/article/is-meditation-overrated/
http://link.springer.com/article/10.1023/B:COTR.0000045557.15923.96
http://archinte.jamanetwork.com/article.aspx?articleid=1809754

3. Meditation reduces stress and anxiety. A study from the University of Wisconsin-Madison indicates that the practice of Meditation reduces the grey-matter density in areas of the brain related to anxiety and stress. The individuals who participated in the study were more able to attend moment-to-moment to the stream of stimuli to which they were exposed to and less likely to 'get stuck' on any one stimulus.

This means that when we monitor non-reactively the contents of experience from moment-to-moment, primarily as a means to recognize the nature of emotional and cognitive patterns but also as a mean to better understand some fundamental truths about the nature of our minds, we reduce the apprehension of future events. Along the way, we reduce stress and anxiety!

http://www.ncbi.nlm.nih.gov/pmc/articles/PMC2944261/
http://onlinelibrary.wiley.com/doi/10.1002/da.21964/abstract;jsessionid=287E5428C871ECEFB6DDC81FB5DCCD80.f04t04

4. Meditation helps reduce symptoms of panic disorder. In a research published in the American Journal of Psychiatry, 22 patients diagnosed with anxiety or panic disorders were submitted to a 3 months meditation and relaxation training. As a result, for 20 of those patients, the effects of panic and anxiety had reduced substantially and the changes were maintained at follow-up.

5. Meditation increases grey matter concentration in the brain. A group of Harvard neuroscientists ran an experiment where 16 people were submitted to an eight-week mindfulness course, using guided meditations and integration of mindfulness into everyday activities. At the end of it, MRI scans showed that the grey matter concentration increased in areas of the brain involved in learning and memory but also in regulating emotions, sense of self, and perspective. In other words, if we cultivate a regular practice, our perspective on life's circumstances and experience becomes more faithful to the way things really are.

6. Meditation improves your focus, attention, and ability to work under stress. A study led by The University of California suggests that during and after a meditation training, subjects were more skilled at keeping focus, especially on repetitive and boring tasks.

Another study demonstrated that even with only 20 minutes a day of practice, students were able to improve their performance on tests involving cognitive skill, in some cases doing 10 times better than another group that did not meditate.

They also performed better on information-processing tasks that were designed to induce deadline stress. In fact, there is evidence that meditators have a thicker prefrontal cortex and right anterior insula, and to this effect, the practice might offset the loss of cognitive abilities associated with old age.

7. Meditation improves information processing and decision-making. A study done at the UCLA Laboratory of Neuro-Imaging suggest that long-term meditators have larger amounts of gyrification ("folding" of the cortex) than people who do not meditate.

Scientists suspect that gyrification is responsible for making the brain better at processing information, making decisions, forming memories and improving attention.
http://newsroom.ucla.edu/releases/evidence-builds-that-meditation-230237

8. Meditation gives you mental strength, resilience, and emotional intelligence. PhD psychotherapist Dr. Ron Alexander reports in his book Wise Mind, Open Mind that the process of controlling the mind, through meditation, increases mental strength, resilience, and emotional intelligence.
http://www.amazon.com/Wise-Mind-Open-Finding-
Purpose/dp/157224643X/ref=as_li_qf_sp_asin_il_tl?tag=livanddar-20

9. Meditation increases your ability to keep focus in spite of distractions. A study from Emory University, Atlanta, demonstrated that participants with more meditation experience exhibit increased connectivity within the brain networks controlling attention.

These neural relationships may be involved in the development of cognitive skills, such as maintaining attention and disengaging from distraction.

Moreover, the benefits of the practice were observed also in normal states of consciousness during the day, which speaks to the transference of cognitive abilities "off the cushion" into daily life.
http://www.clinph-journal.com/article/S1388-2457(13)01228-5/abstract?cc=y

Q&A

Below you will find questions that were asked to me by during seminars, coaching sessions, but also on twitter and email. Some of the questions and answers are verbatim. Others are generic, which is to say that I combined certain types of questions that were frequently asked into one, and extracted the essence from different answers to form one generic answer. I hope you find them – both questions and answers – insightful.

Q. I have a system in which I have done a considerable amount of testing [both back testing and in forward testing]. The system is a positive expectancy one; however, I am still a "scratch" trader. I exercise and meditate on a regular basis. Is there anything which fundamentally needs to change?

A. If your system has been proven to work in the past, then I think it's fair to assume that it has an equal chance of working in the future – assuming that the past holds any kind of predictive value, which I believe it does. Now that this is out of the way, do you execute that edge flawlessly? If you do, then it's just a matter of time before the probabilities start working in your favor. Trade small and often, that's all I can add. If you don't trade your edge flawlessly, then try to figure out what is preventing you from doing so.

Fear, greed – these states only exist within the confines of our own minds. When you realize this, you also realize that you don't have to act on these thoughts, bodily sensations, and emotions. That is why I think that meditation is THE exercise that all traders should incorporate in their daily routine because it allows them to cultivate a sense of detachment from whatever they are feeling. One is not the fear or the greed that he/she feels anymore, one is merely an observer of it.

You already meditate, and that is amazing! I cannot state enough how much meditation has helped me in my journey as a trader. Hang in there! If you have come to a point in your trading where you basically break even, you have already distanced yourself from the crowd. Now it's just a matter of refining a few things here and there and you will be well on your way to profitability.

Q. You say you don't have any credentials in psychology, but how did you learn all this? And how can I trust you to guide me in the right direction if you don't have any certificate to attest that the knowledge you are imparting is accurate?

A. What I talk about is a function of the kind of breakthroughs I've had as a result of my humble encounters with my own mind. If you want to live a better life, there are some truths to be known about the human condition and those truths are available for anyone to learn.

The character of this conversation we are constantly having with ourselves is, by and large, what engineers our unhappiness and the mediocrity of our lives in the present moment. Thoughts and emotions arise in consciousness the way clouds appear in the blue sky. It is the over-identification with these discursive appearances that prevents us from trading with a carefree state of mind.

There are some complex books out there that have been written on the subject of trading psychology that are more confusing than anything. But the subject doesn't have to be that complicated. The only reason why this is so difficult for most is because we aren't taught to investigate our thoughts, emotions and feelings from a young age, as a way to understand ourselves and better deal with our pain and sufferings. In fact, we are usually taught the exact opposite – that our mind is a mysterious place that can only be understood by experts (psychologists).

We are taught to suppress what we feel in such a way that it becomes toxic to us. We become slaves to some dysfunctional beliefs that we unavoidably acquire and those become the filters through which we see the world. We become chained to our thoughts and emotions, and this shapes the way we experience our lives.

In anything that I share, I am not making any claims about the neurophysiological events happening in the brain. What I talk about is merely a matter of subjective experience which you can observe in the laboratory of your own life with a little bit of introspection and mindfulness.

Q. *Do I have to become a Buddhist to practice meditation?*

A. The practice of meditation does not ask us to become a Buddhist or a religious person. We don't have to become Muslims to study algebra, do we? Even though Muslims invented algebra, it is a secular field in its own right. Similarly, when we study physics, do we refer to it as Christian physics? No. Even though Christians invented physics, we merely refer to it as physics. So, a contemplative practice like meditation doesn't require us to get interested in – or espouse – Buddhism... or any other eastern religion. It's just a means to an end. Meditation is merely brain exercises. That's how I see it.

Q. *How do I know that I'm meditating the right way?*

A. There are two ways to approach this question:
1.   If at any point during your practice, you notice that you are lost in thoughts and you consciously and compassionately reroute your attention to the sensations of your breath, you are doing it "right."

2.   If you notice that you feel more patient, calm, and if you are noticing any qualitative changes in your trading experience, more so in your life, in general, I think it's very reasonable to state that your meditation practice is going well. So this is something that you will have to explore by yourself.

Q. I really like how articulate you are on the subject of trading psychology. Your perspective on this is really refreshing especially since you talk from personal experience. But I still don't understand what you mean by "cultivating equanimity." Can you elaborate a little bit on this – why is it so important?

A. In its strictest sense "equanimity" means calmness, composure, even-mindedness. However, I use the word equanimity in my first book, to describe something greater than that – it's the ability to sink beneath our incessant thoughts, even for a few seconds at a time, and act from this place of inner calmness, stillness, and peace.

While I don't always succeed towards my intention of cultivating equanimity in trading, and other areas in my life (like everyone else), equanimity is a concept I strive for as much as possible. And here's a tip: the more you practice this, the better you get at it, and of course, the happier and peaceful you become.

Trading is not easy. We, traders, are not guaranteed financial rewards for every trade we place. It's actually very often the opposite, however, in response, we have one of two choices:

We can respond with anger, frustration, despair, anxiety, and in some cases even animosity. This, however, has the unfortunate side effect of making us feel really bad, in addition to making the situation much worse than it is because nobody can perform to the best of their abilities in such conditions.

Or

We can accept the nature of the game, remain positive, and cultivate equanimity – which is definitely the best option. This is the choice I try to take in all cases. This philosophy of remaining positive applies to all parts of life, not just to trading.

Q. *Will meditation work on me?*

A. Meditation will work on anyone who has a functioning human nervous system. All you need is an equally functioning brain to follow the simple instructions I have outlined in this book.

Q. *I can't seem to sustain a regular meditation practice, even though I know its importance, especially for us traders. Any tips on how to get over this issue?*

A. Here are two reasons why I think people are unable to sustain a regular meditation practice:

1. The awareness of how we are lost in thoughts 99% of the time is, I think, the first reason. What's interesting is how so many people reflexively think that their mind is somehow busier than everyone else's. Welcome to the human condition. Everyone's mind is busy! The key is to stop resisting thoughts and trying to make them go away.

Thoughts are a natural activity in the mind. Although meditation can be a way to experience inner silence, this comes about not by eliminating thoughts but by becoming aware of the silence that is naturally present beneath those thoughts.

2. People don't meditate the right way hence, they don't see the results, and then they quit. To enjoy the benefits of meditation you have to do it properly – sitting with your eyes closed and thinking is, unfortunately, not meditation!

Not being able to stick with a consistent meditation practice is a result of the thoughts you are identifying with. So here is my suggestion: start with an incredibly small practice of 5 minutes a day. As you get more and more comfortable with practicing for 5 minutes, add an increment of 2 minutes. Keep doing that until you have a practice of at least 15-20 minutes a day. And if you slip, be compassionate towards yourself and get back on track. Above all, be patient with yourself.

Q. I don't have time to meditate...

A. There's an old Zen saying that goes like this: *"You should sit in meditation 20 minutes a day; unless you're too busy or you don't have time, then you should sit for an hour."*

If you knew that there was a better life waiting for you as a result of cultivating that regular meditation practice; better trading results, better appreciation of the present moment, liberation from your worries... would you find the time? I'll let you reflect on that!

Q. *Any tips on how to start off my session on the right foot?*

A. What I have found that works is having a very clear start in your practice, with a strong intention. I now make the following part of my routine: when I sit down, I take three very long breath. I breathe in through the nose (filling my lungs to the brim) and out through the mouth (emptying them fully). Then I say to myself in the privacy of my own mind: *"At this moment, I am not interested in anything else in this universe. I'm not interested in any thought, memory or feeling. I'm only interested in this practice. During this time, there is nothing more for me to think or do — only this!"*

Q. *I can't seem to focus on the breath without trying to control it. Any tips?*

A. This is a very normal thing to happen in the beginning. Let it be. Give it some time. Just keep observing without the intention of changing it. If anything changes anyways, that's fine, but don't do it intentionally. Be aware of the breath changing. That is enough.

Q. Is there a difference between introspection and meditation?

A. In its strictest sense, no. But I like to think that there is a difference between the two. The way I see it, introspection involves active thought processes and investigation of your thoughts, emotions, and memories. In other words, content matters!

Meditation/ mindfulness (just semantics), may turn up thoughts, emotions, and memories, but that is not the point. The content is irrelevant. Being able to watch the thoughts and emotions arise and pass away is more important. You specifically want to dis-identify with the thoughts and emotions that arise.

Q. You talk about the benefits of spirituality and mindfulness meditation for traders, but what about other activities that can also be described as spiritual, like for example, playing or listening to music, surf, sports, or any other intellectual endeavor?

A. They are all beneficial because they all involve paying close attention to the present in a way that allows you to be one with whatever you are doing. However, the benefits of meditation are that you don't have to get a guitar, put on your running shoes, wait for a wave, or get yourself an ipod. You can just sit anywhere and pay attention to the most mundane thing ever – the breath. And meditation, I argue, is not just something that provides a little bit of relaxation, focus, peace... it is a radical tool that can help you make some life changing discoveries about the nature of your own mind.

Q. I meditate on a regular basis, and I have certainly seen changes in the way I address my psychological deficiencies when I am faced with a loss. But I feel I am still subject to being disappointed whenever the markets don't accommodate me. Any suggestions on how to decrease the emotional response?

A. Look within yourself to check if you have become emotionally dependent on the markets. Ask yourself the following questions:

- Am I trading as a way to make myself happy?
- Does it upset me if the markets don't act or respond in a certain way?
- Do I complain a lot when I lose, or when the markets don't act the way I would have expected?

If you answered with yes to several of these questions, it may be a sign that you are overly reliant on the markets for well-being, and it could be an indication that you are in need of change. We are often conditioned to seek happiness outside of ourselves. After all, much of the world's economy revolves around the cycle of generating and satisfying needs with things. But we have to realize that if we wait for the markets – or anything that is outside of us – to fulfill us on a moment to moment basis, trading will always be frustrating and a never satisfying endeavor.

If we can find a well-being within us that is not contingent upon the ups and downs of the markets, then we will free our minds in the midst of anything that may incapacitate us and cause us to suffer. This will also free our potential as traders – but also as individuals.

So what I will suggest is to keep your practice of meditation and self-awareness. When something bad is happening to us in the markets, we almost always feel identical to the experience. We don't think that this is only happening in our heads. Meditation is merely a means to continually draw back into this state of merely witnessing everything that is arising. How could these mental occurrences be what you are? You are merely noticing them. How is it that you feel identical to this voice you hear in your head? This is merely an illusion. When you acknowledge this, you become able to be more present in your life and with your experiences.

Also, I would suggest that you stay engaged in the markets. When you trade a lot, you build and refine your skills as a trader. Remember, just like in anything: practice makes perfect! But to keep practicing – to stay in the game – you have to trade small so as not to make ruin a feasible outcome for you.

Q. Sometimes I feel discourages by my lack of progress in trading. Any idea on how to get over this?

A. Too often we, traders, are hard on ourselves, especially at the beginning of our career. We feel bad about our lack of progress, we feel guilty that we haven't been as disciplined as we wish we could have been, and we regret the actions we took.

My view on this is that this is a strange case of looking at the glass half empty, and this kind of thinking almost certainly hinders our progress.

Here's what I propose instead: Look back and see what you've done so far, and feel proud of your progress. Be happy about how far you've come so far, even if you still have a long way to go. Appreciate your accomplishments. Okay, you might have screwed up on a few trades this month, but at least you entered those trades. You can only learn by trading; by being active, by making mistakes. No matter how much you repeat those mistakes over and over again, you will eventually learn, until comes a time when you won't make those mistakes again. You see what I mean? Look at the glass as half full.

For example, you might think that I've achieved a lot as a trader, but as you read in this book, it took me a lot of time to become consistently profitable. I am a slow learner, and there were plenty of times when I felt discouraged. There were times when I felt miserable and defeated. Those were times when all the progress I made went to pieces. The worst I felt, the most I would act upon those feelings in the markets, like a self-fulfilling prophecy.

The key is to step back and look back on what you've done. Sure, you might have screwed up a couple of times, but look at how much progress you've done so far. Look at where you are today. Don't buy into those bad feelings, they're lying to you. Instead of beating yourself up, celebrate your current successes, no matter how small!

We will always feel guilty about what we have or haven't done, but it is important that we remind ourselves that it is only a temporary setback. I always tell myself that it's just a small bump on a long road. Take the long view, both behind you and ahead of you. You are exactly where you need to be.

Q. What are the effects meditation has had on your ability to trade?

A. The first thing I started noticing is how impatient I was when I traded, so meditation gave me the actual extra push to inquire more about what I felt and instead observe. Who is feeling impatient? Why? How does it feel? Same thing when I felt fear. Who is feeling fear?

When you ask those questions it becomes clear to you that you have the choice of acting (or not) on those thoughts and feelings because you are not them anymore, you are merely an observer.

Also, meditation has allowed me to be more accepting of losses and of things I can't control like market action, a specific outcome, news, etc. And there are much more benefits but I think you get the point. Meditation is a must for all traders!

Q. How long will it take for me to see the results of my practice?

A. My practice, at first, was solely centered on the expectation of having something in return – better mental clarity, judgment, capacity to take fast and rational decisions, to handle stress, etc. These are all areas in which meditation helps with, however, little did I know that the act of expecting something in return instantly took me out of the experience of the present moment. In other words, when we practice meditation with the expectation of obtaining something from it in the future, we are already lost in thoughts and that which we expect has fewer chances of happening.

Science has confirmed to us the benefits of having a regular meditation practice, and we should visualize those benefits as potential goals... but then we should release them! The path – your daily practice – is the goal.

Q. How long should I keep my meditation practice?

A. Meditation has changed my life for the better. In fact after only a few weeks of meditating and experiencing this 'new way', I realized that life without it felt more chaotic, overwhelming and stressful.

The important thing to note from my experience is that while I knew I was stressed and overwhelmed before by my failures in the markets, it took meditation to uncover the extent of it. The practice increased my self-awareness, but most importantly, gave me a better balance in life and in trading by helping me manage my thoughts and emotions, and by helping me develop equanimity.

If you want durable results, you have to make it a life-long commitment. There is no way around. Success (in and out of the markets), well-being, those are causal states, which is to say that they are a direct result of a daily process.

BONUS

PARADIGM SHIFT
How To Cultivate Equanimity In The Face Of Market Uncertainty

CHAPTER 1 -- THE START

"If you wish to know the road, inquire of those who have travelled it"
~ *Japanese proverb*

The ability to manage thoughts and emotions with the end goal of remaining calm and balanced under pressure has a direct link to performance.1 I wish I was aware of that when I decided to quit my day job and trade for a living. It would have prevented me from making some costly (and painful) mistakes because I would have probably taken more time to reflect on whether to take the leap of faith or not. But the reality of life is that things don't always happen the way we would want them to.

My interest for the financial markets started when I was in my teenage years. I remember my older brother showing me a financial website and eagerly saying "people actually make a living buying and selling stocks on a regular basis, you know". Naturally, I was struck with curiosity so I started researching more on the subject. Those were the early days of the internet, and trading-related information wasn't readily accessible within the click of a mouse, nor was it as inexpensive (or free) as it is nowadays. Yet, I did find enough information to further spark my interest, firmly planting the trading/ investing seed inside my head.

I remember being so fascinated, from such a young age, by compound return tables, quotes, and market-related news. At that time, making money in the markets surely seemed easy – just like a low hanging fruit waiting to be plucked. So I thought!

A couple of years later, I had saved a rather significant amount of money from various jobs I took throughout the years and I went on to invest it all with a buy and hold approach. Despite the favorable market conditions during that period, I ended up losing money, which led me to the conclusion that the buy and hold approach is ultimately a game of chance.

And the reason is simple: this "strategy" never addresses some fundamental questions one needs to know before putting one's hard earned money at work. These are just a couple of those questions:

"Buying how much of what?"

"At what price?"

"Holding for how long?"

"Do you ever sell? If so, how and when?"

"How do you make money in a bear market?"

So by definition, the buy and hold approach doesn't fit into a positive expectancy mold.

Unfortunately, by the time I realized this I had already lost a good portion of my investment capital. However, through my drive to figure out what works and what doesn't, I had amassed enough knowledge to slowly transition to trading on a shorter time frame, which I thought was better suited to my personality and overall aspirations. This shift in timeframe and underlying methodology has also helped me better define my edge in the markets and allowed me to create a significant number of trade occurrences. More on this later.

From there, you could be inclined to think that it was all smooth sailing for me. I wish I could tell you that! Before I was able to engineer consistency, first in my behavior, and then my trading results, I went through significant drawdowns – both emotional and financial.

I made all the mistakes you could possibly imagine, from trading with "scared money" to changing methodologies like one changes underwear... And those difficult but highly instructive times eventually made me realize that success in the markets is 100% psychology! Some people like to view the system, risk management and psychology components as equal. Some like to give greater importance to risk and money management. But personally, I really think that psychology is the determining factor and deserves top attention. No amount of durable success will come to you in the markets if you can't act in your own best interest.

Without the right psychology, even the most robust system is doomed to failure. Similarly, risk and money management will only assure "death by a thousand paper cuts", supposing one can get to the point where one can efficiently manage risk in the first place. Regardless of the kind of positive expectancy your system displays, if you are unable to follow your rules and execute your trades properly with minimal trading errors, you will surely find trading to be an exasperating endeavor.

The right psychology also encompasses the appropriate work ethics. Trading – or I should say successful trading – requires a lot of work, dedication, and sacrifice at first. Honestly, I must admit that I am happy that things are that way. If things were easier everyone – neighbors, uncles, grandmothers – would be successful traders and make a killing in the markets. There would be no challenge, no fulfillment, and no desire to achieve. In other words, the world would be a very boring place.

When we conquer difficulty, we manufacture for ourselves an immense feeling of satisfaction. When something is difficult, overcoming it feels like a real triumph and this creates an amazing experience. A positive feedback loop when activated generally begets more success. This is because though the challenges may seem impossible at first glance, with repetition we will begin to see patterns arise in the chaos, and we will find that things aren't so difficult after all if we take the time to analyze the problem at hand.

So, in the face of difficulty, what is left for us to do, in terms of an attitude to adopt, is to adapt. Many won't! But rest assured that all the successful traders and great achievers out there have done it at one point.

Successful trading can only happen when you have sorted out the resistances that are preventing you from making money on a consistent basis – and we'll define what consistency is later in the book. Paradoxically, when you have sorted out these resistances, you become someone else. If you came in solely for the money at first, you might find out that this isn't the unique motivator anymore – the game and the challenge it represents is what keeps you in. If you reach this point – and I am hopeful that you do – money will automatically manifest itself to you. Dropping our obsession for money somehow gives us more of it. I will address this point later on as well.

I don't have any credentials in psychology, however, just like many others before me I learned most of what I discuss in this book through repeated mistakes, painful losses, and failures. We evolve in a world where we are led to believe that the mental environment is a perplexing and peculiar place that can only be understood by experts (psychologists). As a result, most people end up living their lives in a way that lacks any conspicuous understanding as to the relationship between their mind and the outer physical world – markets included. This lack of understanding ultimately shapes the way they experience their lives, in and out of the markets.

We don't need a Ph.D. to understand the nature of our own mind. We just have to make ourselves available to learning more about the nature of our dissatisfactions – and few people are truly willing to do that. They would rather attempt to change the outer physical world in order to fit what is inside of them and quite often this will turn out to be a futile endeavor, especially in the markets. It was only when I started to realize this, by means of deeply questioning myself, that I began to see dramatic shifts in the way I perceived the market, but also in the way I perceived myself and life in general.

This is so because questions asked the right way usually point to their own answers. If one does not ask the right questions, one cannot expect to get the right answers. Markets don't hurt us. It is our own sets of beliefs that condition us to suffer whenever the markets don't oblige us by fulfilling our needs. It is our beliefs that cause us to overthink when a trade has to be entered or exited. They also cause us to doubt ourselves and our ability to trade successfully.

Eager to deepen my understanding of myself and how I essentially created my own pain and suffering in trading (but also in my personal life), I began spending a lot of time meditating. I attended several meditation retreats and solo wilderness expeditions where I had some life-changing encounters with my own mind.

A spiritual practice like meditation can teach us a lot of things about the nature of the being, to some extent the nature of reality, and above all the transiency and ever-changing nature of everything that exists – markets included. It can help us understand, more so accept, change as an intrinsic part of our lives, and that is precisely a quality that is needed in the markets.

With a better understanding of myself, came a better understanding of the markets. It all began to make sense after a while – I was desperately trying to force the markets to conform to whatever beliefs I had, in terms of what I thought I deserved, what I believed I was entitled to, whatever special trading talent I thought I had, and so on. Once I targeted those problem thoughts and beliefs; and once I started developing a new relationship with my emotions, trading took a whole new direction for me. My results finally came in line with my new expectations.

Developing equanimity was a long and tedious process for me, however, once I acquired it the repercussions went far beyond market success. My whole life was changed. It's as if my vision of life went from a boring 8-bit video game to a sophisticated new generation 3D game, and there is a reason for that. Markets are not different from life itself. Comparing the two, we can see that:

• Markets and life are both uncertain. We cannot know for sure what will happen on a period to period basis. Both are "games" of probabilities.

• They both provide us with opportunities. We can decide to be bold and bet the farm on every occasion, or we can be methodical in our approach and make calculated moves. Either way, if you don't bet – if you don't take risks – you can't play.

• If we are unprepared we can feel pain and suffering as a result of not being able to flow with them or accept their reality.

• At every corner, they can teach us a lesson if we are open to it.

... the comparisons can go on and on, therefore, it is not difficult to see how the skills, habits, or even delusions you acquire in one can often impact how you behave in the other. That is why developing equanimity becomes primordial because if you can effectively transform the way you behave when faced with difficult situations in the markets, I believe you can definitely affect the way you behave when you're equally faced with difficult life circumstances.

A good approach to trading, I argue, is a way of living, and developing equanimity is a big part of that process. Equanimity is not a word that is commonly used, and its signification for me is beyond mental calmness or composure. It is the radical non-interference with the natural flow of sensory experiences. For example, if emotions are arising in your body as a result of sensory stimulation (what you hear or see) in the markets, you are not trying to hold onto those emotions nor are you trying to push them down, whatever those emotions are. Instead, you take an observer stance and you watch them arise, and because of their transient and impermanent nature, they slowly fade away. By practicing equanimity, you learn not to react. At any given moment, you don't allow your past mental conditioning to take possession of your present actions, and since you give no stimulation to the mind in that regard, you don't reinforce such conditioning and you don't generate new future ones. This sense of detachment or as the French say "sang froid", allows you to take the right action in regards to circumstances and conditions that are happening. It is the end of the ego.

Lots of different people view the end of the ego in different ways. Others find such a statement nonsensical. The way I see it is that the end of the ego is just equanimity. It is the end of craving and attachment. It's a way of observing yourself and your environment without any filters; it's seeing things for what they truly are beneath our fixed beliefs, values, thoughts, emotions.

I won't lie, this state, once reached, is hard to sustain because our mind's goal is to think – about the past and the future. But, the amazing thing is that equanimity can be summoned over and over again throughout the day, and especially during trading, even for a few moment at a time, and this is the all-too-important difference!

We all have experienced at some point a gap between what we realize as possible in terms of results from our trading, and what our current bottom line is. This happens because we can't seem to restrict ourselves from doing things that aren't in our best interest. Most of us are stuck at this stage and unable to figure out how to change things. This is where equanimity comes in handy – and it is achievable by anyone, but it requires a genuine and sincere willingness to learn how to do it. And this requires practice, practice.... and some more practice.

Throughout the book, I will refer to my contemplative experience in order to shed light on the various aspects of unsuccessful trading and what I think is its antidote. My intention is not to fill this book with mumbo jumbo new age religious ideologies – though, good trading, as said before, does require equanimity, which means reconnecting with your inner-self; paying attention to the nature of your mind, and beholding the environment you evolve in for what it truly is. In simple terms, it's the essence of spirituality.

Spirituality needs not to have religious connotations. "Spirit" comes from the Latin word "to breathe", and it typically involves a search for meaning in life. When you breathe mindfully and turn your attention inwards; when you grasp the intricacy, beauty, and subtlety of life, in the midst of vicissitudes, then that soaring feeling, that sense of elation and humility combined, is surely spiritual.

I only aspire to help you realize your potential, not only as a trader but also as an individual. I will give you a very detailed and comprehensive blue-print on how to develop equanimity. I will show you how to bring more consistency into your trading and into your life. While I cannot promise you that you will make money, I guarantee you that you will become a better trader and overall a better "you" if you understand and follow the principles I discuss about.

TRADING: A REAL BUSINESS

Anyone who starts down the road to becoming a trader wants to reach consistency in their results as fast as possible, but few eventually make it there. In fact, several studies2 suggest that most retail traders are worse off financially after the first couple of years in the financial markets than before they started trading – i.e. if they make it through those early years without going broke in the first place. This is a staggering truth and one that is seared onto most traders' brains at this point since we keep hearing about the high failure rate in this field. Naturally, this begs the question: why do so many people fail in the markets?

Retail traders – those who trade or aspire to trade for a living – are by the very definition self-employed. To succeed as a self-employed trader you need two very distinct skill-sets: first as a self-employed business owner, and second as a professional trader. Both skills work in unison, one cannot be without the other. Therefore, it's not hard to see that for some, trading might not be a good fit at all because it initially requires a lot of work.

Trading is a real business though few actually treat it as such. In fact, any activity engaged on a regular basis with the intent of making money is a business! So, approaching our trading operations from a business standpoint means that:

1. We have to develop a concept or an idea which aims to satisfy a market inefficiency, diversify risk and make money work for us.

2. We have to test that idea and see how it performs over time.

3. We have to hold an inventory. This is our current positions. We have to buy them for less than what we intend to sell them for.

4. We have to manage our employees. Our current positions can also be seen as our employees. We have to keep the ones that are working well and fire the ones that aren't.

5. We have to take insurance. Our business must have insurance to manage risk because losses will occur. It is not a matter of "if"; it is a matter of "when". Therefore, stop-losses, hedges and position sizing are our insurance against big losses in our trading business.

6. We have to make strategic deployment of capital. We attempt to buy things at a lower price than what we intend to sell them at. We also try to diversify what we buy so that our risks are uncorrelated and dispersed.

7. We have to conduct our business where there are ample buyers and sellers so that we don't get stuck with positions (inventories) that no one wants.

8. We have to actively preserve our capital. If we lose that we are out of business. Therefore, we have to make sure that we do not go "all in" on any perceived opportunity.

9. We have to work towards the expansion of our business. This means two things: Firstly, it can mean trading more vehicles, perhaps trying a new strategy, and/or adding more trading capital to our accounts so that we can increase the size of our trades. The only caveat is that this can only happen after we become profitable. Secondly, the markets, unfortunately, cannot accommodate us all the time, so it is useful to find other ways of generating income so as to smooth our revenue curve. Offering courses, coaching sessions, mentoring, selling books... all these things are alternative ways of generating income for your trading business.

All these steps have to be figured out on paper prior to starting your trading business through a process called trading plan development. Engaging with the markets with an abstract idea or vague concept of what we should be doing doesn't work! And this is the all-too-common thing people do. It is essential that you develop a trading plan.

We all want security, a reliable source of income and wealth generation, but how can one expect consistent results from any business that never got properly organized in the first place? This is the primary reason why venture capitalists will not even listen to the best of business ideas if the person presenting them doesn't have a well-defined business plan. The underlying assumption is that if you can't build it on paper, how do you expect to build it in the real world?
For this same reason the trading plan is an absolute must for any aspiring trader.

Besides serving you as a support to describe the inner workings of your business, the trading plan is another way of acknowledging the fact that you can't predict the future. Correspondingly, it is there to help you take a structured approach to the markets' uncertainty. Your trading process is not an abstract concept anymore – it becomes well structured. Your rules and processes are clear on paper, all you have to do is execute.

UNCONCIOUS INCOMPETENCE

Setting up a business is one thing, and it can be considered as the easy part. But being mentally prepared to make the business consistently profitable is another thing. While this might be a shocker for a lot of you, it is without a doubt the most challenging aspect of this whole endeavor. For instance, a novice trader may have devised a trading plan and figured out her trading methodology, however, there might still be a negative correlation between what she ends up with and what she could have had. In other words, for some reason, she might not be using her methodology to its full potential.

Just as buying a car won't give us the ability to actually drive it, novice traders erroneously believe that with the creation (or buying) of their own methodology comes the intrinsic skills to actually trade it flawlessly. They do not think that just like with anything they need a particular set of skills in order to exploit their methodology to its full potential.

We cannot take for granted that because we recognize an opportunity to enrich ourselves in some way or another that we will have the skills to be able to take advantage of that opportunity appropriately. But that is exactly what most of us assume at first when we start out. We want to be able to produce an income or a return from our trading that we can rely on, but this is not so much of an easy task as one might be inclined to think. Consistent returns in trading are a result of the consistency in our behavior.

The general public is attracted to the markets because it seems like an easy way to make a lot of money. This leads us to the following paradox propounded by Jack Schwager in one of his Market Wizards book series3. Suppose a layperson decides to become a surgeon. He goes into a bookstore, heads straight to the medical book section, and finds a book entitled "How to perform heart surgery." After spending a couple of days studying it, do you think he would be ready to perform heart surgery? I think we would all agree that even the bare thought of him doing this is preposterous.

Now, suppose that same person decides to go instead in the finance book section of the store, and there he buys a book called "How to beat the market in 7 days." After spending a weekend reading it, suppose he opens up a brokerage account the following week and starts trading with the belief that he can beat the markets on a consistent basis. Do you still think this is utterly ridiculous? You see, it takes years to build a successful trading career, still most people won't see anything odd about that second option.

Trading is probably the world's only profession where a complete amateur – a person who knows absolutely nothing – has a 50 percent chance of being right in the beginning. I haven't seen this phenomenon in any other profession. In trading there are only two things we can do: either we buy or we sell. Naturally, some people are just going to get it right by pure luck at least a few times in the beginning. And, this deceives them into believing that they possess the appropriate skills to trade efficiently. It makes them believe that they have some kind of special talent to predict market directions, or that trading is a lot easier than what it seems. However, the reality is that winning in the markets requires absolutely no skills at all.

Additionally, we don't have to have a good reason – or any reason at all – to put our cursor on the buy or sell button, but doing so, we could immediately find ourselves in a winning trade – and it could be a huge one. Therefore, the natural tendency is to think that if it is this easy to win, it can't be that much harder to make a steady income. The truth is that winning and being a consistent winner are two completely different things, and this can be a really hard mental barrier to break for most.

What novice traders don't understand is that good trading requires skills that need to be developed. Since those skills are counter-intuitive by their very nature, since they tend to go against normal human tendencies, they will have to be developed and built through engagement and practice. What may be expected from such alterations of our normal human tendencies if practiced, developed, often repeated, and well-perfected is mastery over the "self" and its various impulses and afflictive conditions – i.e. anxiety, fear, greed, craving, and so on. You are not overcome by these states but you subdue them as they arise.

New traders who are just starting out in their trading journey should keep in mind the possibilities online trading has to offer, not only in terms of monetary gains but also in terms of personal development. The problem is that they tend to focus too much on the potential monetary rewards and this is what messes up their results because their expectations are not in line with the way markets are.

As you start out in this journey, your attention should be on the adoption of a business-like approach to trading so that you can bring a little more formality and structure to your entire trading operation. You should also acknowledge your current lack of skills to trade the markets effectively. By acknowledging this – by saying, "I am not a consistently profitable trader, yet!" you open yourself to accept new pertinent information to help you grow into the person you need to become in order to return consistent results from your trading operations.

You shouldn't expect to instantly make a comfortable living at home, in your pajamas. You shouldn't expect to be a millionaire by the end of the year. While these scenarios are definitely a possibility, they are highly unlikely to happen right from the get-go. Yet, you can improve your chances of those happening at some later point throughout your trading career by taking the time to prepare now.

'Skills over money' should be the beginner's motto. If you keep an open mind filled with childlike curiosity, and if you cultivate an eagerness to learn and build your skills instead of putting your attention right away on the monetary rewards, you will be far ahead of the crowd.

When your roles and goals as traders and business owner are clearly defined, you can focus on the pure execution of your trading model. However, if you don't clearly define those parameters, then you will have a tendency to act in a way that lacks any kind of structure. This lack of structure is the reason why most retail traders set themselves up for failure right from the start.

CONSCIOUS INCOMPETENCE

When an inspiring trader starts to develop awareness about his incompetence (usually through significant losses) and realizes that there is more work involved in trading than what he originally had I mind, he usually starts to work on finding some kind of Holy Grail/ no fail trading system. It's very easy to get stuck in this stage, but at one point, if that trader is perseverant enough, he will eventually realize that there isn't such a thing as an infallible and ever-winning trading system. The true key to durable market success is a profound understanding of how his state of mind will, in essence, undermine him more often than not.

When this shift in perception (or paradigm) happens, it creates an avalanche of conflicting feelings for the trader. He knows the potential is there to enrich himself beyond his wildest dreams – the markets provide us with that opportunity at every moment. The trader can clearly see his success right before his eyes, however, something within him seems to disrupt his ability to reach for it.

The market represents a challenge, and for many traders, the challenge is also occurring within. Fixed beliefs and values combine with unacknowledged thoughts and unmanaged emotions, driving behavior, which results in mediocre market performance. As "conscious incompetents", such traders realize that they are not as "expert" as perhaps they thought they were when they first started out. The transition from an unconscious incompetent to a conscious competent can initially be shocking, especially if it happens abruptly through severe and significant losses.

This is a very difficult stage to be in because it is where judgments and doubts on oneself's own ability to succeed are formed. It is where failures tend to be seared into one's brain resulting in an apprehension to trade in the future. Consequently, it is a stage where most people give up. They assume that trading simply requires a special talent that they were unfortunately not born with. However, this very stage is where the real learning can begin for those who are persistent.

GOOD TRADING

What constitutes good trading? Surely, it is not a function of intelligence. If it were, every rocket scientist on this earth would become millionaires simply by trading the markets. Given that this isn't the case, we have to concede that the answer resides elsewhere. A proven system and a risk management technique are important but they mean nothing without the following three ingredients:

1. Engagement. Engagement allows you to acquire knowledge and skills. It also creates opportunities but that doesn't come without risk. We'll explore this further in the following chapter.

2. Adaptability and flexibility in the face of uncertainty. This means that you have to accept changes in the

markets, learn from the mistakes that you will undoubtedly make, and embrace the failures that you will certainly experience.

3. How much self-control you display. You have to exert control over your impulses so that you don't get into low probability trades, bet the farm on any single trade, or let small losers grow out of hand.

Those three points work together and they are all sine qua non. The degree to which you fail to develop or work on these is the degree to which your progress will stagnate.

There is nothing esoteric or even illusory about durable market success. Of course, those who have staying power are the ones who get to experience it, but there is nothing extraordinary about this and it is achievable by anyone. Some people might have a predisposition for better self-control, flexibility, adaptability... and this can be summed up as talent. But to my knowledge, talent indeed helps, but it is not the success factor. Self-control, flexibility, and adaptability are skills the untalented can acquire and improve upon.

It is not easy to face our demons and put a stop to some deeply ingrained patterns of unproductive behaviors. However, I wrote this book with the assumption that you desire your trading success strong enough that you are willing to work through the resistances that stand between you and your goal.

When you boil it down to an essence, change is the only logical result of desire. If you truly desire something, you'll find ways to make and facilitate the change, whatever that might be. Desire, however, is not to be confused with craving. I strongly believe there is a clear distinction between the two. Desire is an expression of longing. The pursuit of that which we desire gives meaning to our lives. On the other hand, craving is an expression of neediness. When we are on autopilot – and thus incognizant – we tend to crave things. When we remain centered in our awareness and consciousness, we can desire things and align our actions with our intentions so that both are in harmony.

Awareness allows us to identify what is truly important to us. Desire leads us forward, craving doesn't! It is the attachment to desire and it is a poison that will consume you. It will cause you to pin your happiness to the very thing you desire in such a way that you will melt into grief if you don't get what you want. Furthermore, craving will impede on your ability to take rational decisions, which will undoubtedly make durable market success an impossibility.

It doesn't matter if you own a clothing store, a fast-food outlet or even an online marketing business… if you want consistent results you have to be consistent in what you do! This is even more essential in a trading business because of the obvious mental afflicts felt in the midst of real-time moving markets. With no structure to the way you approach the markets, you will have a tendency to act impulsively; to feed into fear, frustration, greed, aversion, and thus, reinforce negative patterns of behavior. If you can make it a priority to stay methodical and systematic, you won't be subject to such wild emotional swings that will detract your trading results.

End of the free chapter.
Paradigm Shift is available on Amazon.com

The Next Level

Thanks for reading. Hopefully, you now see that **trading for a living is possible!** It's not just a myth... people actually do this for a living, **and it's very rewarding.**

And I'm confident that anyone can do this. **If you're a "normally functioning" human being with an average intelligence, you can be a trader – and a profitable one.**

I hope I was successful in reflecting back to you some things that may have been out of your perspective. If it is the case, then I think it's fair to say that the reading was worthwhile.

Now, as insightful or revealing as those things were, simply reading isn't enough. **You have to take action.**

I have designed two courses to help you with that.

The first one is called the **Trading Psychology Mastery Course.**

I can tell you, this course is unlike anything you've seen! In it, **I aspire to help you develop into an emotionally intelligent trader**, regardless of your background.

I am a trader with several years of experience in anything pertaining to meditation and present moment awareness (mindfulness).

I have a strong meditation practice; so far, I've spent a cumulative total of about 6 months on intensive silent meditation retreats and I've studied with many renowned "enlightened" teachers and gurus.

Meditation/ Mindfulness have provoked some deep transformations in me and the way I trade. I like to think **that I've now developed a thorough understanding of my mind and I want to help you go through that same process of transformation.**

Rest assured, you don't have to spend a ton of time on intensive silent retreats like I did to go through such changes. **But you have to know what you're doing and you need the guidance of something who doesn't just talk the talk but who walks it, extensively.**

Mindfulness is a simple practice yet deep, but also hazardous if not practice properly or with a right understanding. In this day and age, while it is certainly easy and beneficial to just download a free meditation app and start this way, **there are many pitfalls to the practice and a confirmed meditation instructor will help shepherd you in the right direction.**

Being both an experienced meditator and a profitable trader, I will provide you with the right knowledge and a foundation for insights, and I will guide you in your practice.

I'm not going to rehash things at you. No. We're going to practice together.

Market success begins with stability of mind (thoughts and emotions), flexibility, patience, concentration, and non-attachment, all of which are deeply addressed in this two-week practical and home immersion course. In it you will learn:

• How you create your own results in the markets – good or bad.

- How to work with obstacles, such as our mental conditioning, or your normal propensity for not accepting risk; for wanting to be right, craving certainty, and so on.

- How to detach yourself from the concept of money, for a smoother trading experience.

- How to deepen your concentration.

- How to self-regulate, so that whatever happens in the markets, you'll remain unperturbed, stable, and focused.

- And more...

The following is required of you if you decide to enroll in the course:

- Get yourself a journal.

- Abstinence from any trading activity for 2 weeks.

- Commitment, commitment, commitment!

Very few traders work on developing strong skills of introspection. I know absolutely brilliant people who could have been extraordinary traders if they had cultivated an ability to make the most basic discrimination about their moment to moment experience.

Conversely, I've met many traders who aren't especially brilliant but who are so in tune with themselves that they are unshakable and equanimous in the midst of uncertainty and vicissitudes. **This makes all the difference in terms of market performance!**

The barriers we face in trading are always a function of the stories we tell ourselves. **You will learn to calm your mind and to drop beneath the stories. You will begin to experience your trading in a whole new way.**

Sometimes shifts are dramatic and sometimes gradual, but I will guide you and support you on this path.

If you can commit to the course wholeheartedly, you should start seeing results within a month. **Yes, one month!**

So, enroll if:

- You think you might be up for the challenge (and promise you, it's going to be a challenge!).

- If you want to learn more about yourself. By 'conquering' yourself, you will conquer the markets

- If you are serious about your trading career (and your life)

That being said, I have also devised a second course and it's called the **Trading For A Living Course.** This course is the next step.

In there, I show you my trading strategies, I show you my actual performance -- **the kind of money that I make monthly.**

In short, **in the Trading For A Living Course, you get to see how a profitable trader runs his business from A to Z** (a truly profitable one, not some kind of make-belief "profitable trader" you see online these days).

And I'm doing this not to show off but to inspire you; to show you that it's possible -- **with actual proof.**

You can take my model (my business plan) and apply it

as it is if so desire, or you can take it in an entirely new direction... it's really up to you.

Anyone can trade for a living. I'm not some kind of genius. I have a high school level of education. So yes, you can do this! **I'm able to trade for a living not because of my intelligence or my "no-fail" trading strategies (no strategy ever is fool-proof!), I'm able to do so because my number one priority is conscious emotional management.** In everything that I do; in every action that I take.

Essentially, with both courses, *The Trading psychology mastery Course* and *The Trading For A Living Course*, **you'll learn to be in control of yourself, how to generate a reliable stream of monthly income, and how to build a long-lasting trading career.**

Now, if you decide to get the courses separately, they're both priced at $199 each. But quite frankly, they complement each other very nicely and **they form a complete program for the trader who is serious about trading for a living -- about making it happen.**

And so, I want you to get both courses together, and I'm offering them in a bundle with a discount of 25% ($100 off).

I genuinely want to see you succeed; I want to see you improve your life, make money, and thrive as a human being. Cliché but true...

Head to http://www.tradingcomposure.com to learn more and get started. And if there's anything you want to ask me personally, here's my email tradingcomposureinfo@gmail.com

In closing, here are some reviews for both courses.

Trading Psychology Mastery Course

*"This course was one of many courses and books I researched before investing my time & I am glad I chose this course. It is so practical and sustainable as it helps you create habits for continued success after its completion. I would strongly recommend this course as it has been one of the best investments of my time & money. It has already made a large positive impact on not just my life, happiness, and more, but also, as prescribed my trading + view of markets." ~ **Dan Buehring***

"If you view the material with an open mind, and participate fully in the exercises, this course will change the way you view the world. It has had a positive effect on my relationships, and the way I view myself. After consistently practicing over the last month, I have noticed I have become more creative with my trading. I will wake in the night and write things down in a notebook. This would occasionally happen before, but it is much more frequent since I started my mediation practice. I have had epiphanies about my behavior and its relationship to my ego. By being able to step back from your thoughts, things become clearer. I highly recommend the course. Yvan is an excellent teacher and a person of honor and integrity." ~ **Alan Cooper**

"I have been meditating for past 3 years, but was not able to link it with trading. Searched all over to see how can I apply concepts of meditation to trading. Stumbled upon this by chance and would consider the best accident to happen. Yvan has beautifully designed this course. This course will be last investment in Trading psychology. What makes it more interesting is the concepts taught here are life skills that can be applied in all walks of life." ~ **Shashank Gonchigar**

Trading For A Living Course

"This is by far the most honest trading course you would

*ever come across. It might not only change your whole approach towards trading, it might change you life per se! In the course, Yvan talks about his trading system and has opened up on how he makes a living via trading business. There are enormous amounts of examples which will set you on the path if you trust. He not only talks and provides strategies, he "walks the talk " as well." ~ **Saurabh Srivastav***

*"In this course, Yvan explains how he set up his trading business in a very hands on way. He shows you his own trading strategies, results and how he´s able to sustain a healthy income... I am a big fan of Yvan as he is being very transparent, honest, humble, straight to the point, and will help advise you on how to do this yourself. Yvan does everything in a simple fashion and breaks everything down step by step. There´s never any doubt on what to do, how to do it or where to go to and get it. He will explain everything to you. If you haven´t heard of this guy before, then I can thoroughly recommend you take this course. Besides this course, Yvan has other courses and books out that deals more with trading psychology, which is Yvan´s special field. The guy changed a lot of things in my trading and in my life already, you won´t find a more open "book" than this." ~ **Mikkel Larsen***

"I found the content fantastic with clear & precise instructions on how to implement the systems shown and run a successful trading company. The simplicity of

*the systematic approach in comparison to a discretionary system I was taught and heavily emotionally digested in without realizing, was well and truly breath taking and a pleasure to learn what you had to say. I was amazed at myself and my own beliefs after completing this course and now cannot wait to put to the test what you have shown me." ~ **Craig Sanders**

Head to http://www.tradingcomposure.com

Made in the USA
Coppell, TX
26 October 2023

23421941R00066